SOCIAL STUDIES QUIZ WHIZ

WRITTEN BY
Linda Schwartz

ILLUSTRATED BY
Kelly Kennedy

**The
Learning
Works**

Illustrator: Kelly Kennedy

Book design: Studio E Books, Santa Barbara, CA

Cover illustrator: Rick Grayson

Cover designer: Barbara Peterson

Project director: Linda Schwartz

CONTENTS

The question cards in *Social Studies Quiz Whiz* are grouped into 10 categories of 36 question cards each. In each section you will find 6 folios, each with 6 cards. The 10 categories can be identified by their borders, as shown below:

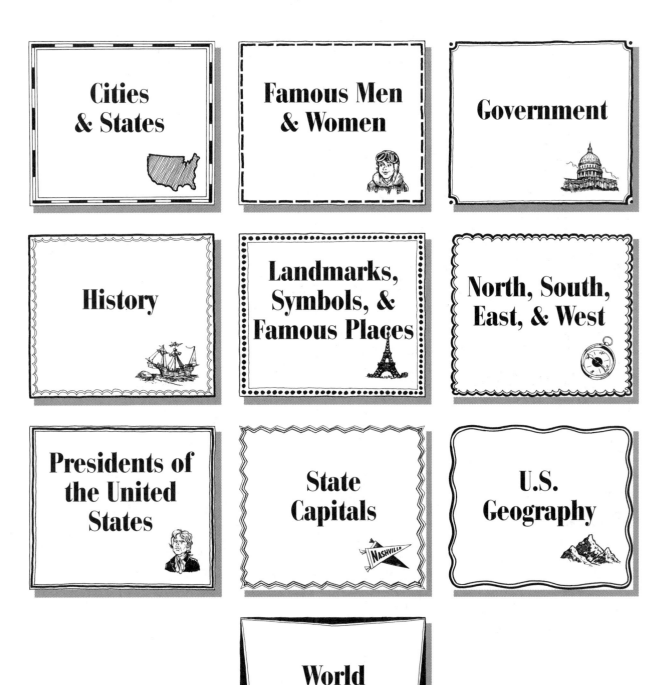

Cities & States

Famous Men & Women

Government

History

Landmarks, Symbols, & Famous Places

North, South, East, & West

Presidents of the United States

State Capitals

U.S. Geography

World Geography

WAYS TO USE
Social Studies Quiz Whiz
IN CLASS

There are numerous ways to use *Social Studies Quiz Whiz* in class. To begin with, you can open the book to any page and ask a few questions to start your morning, to begin a social studies lesson, or to fill those last minutes before lunch, recess, or the end of the day. If you have more time, try one of the following creative ideas.

Quiz Whiz Game

Start by removing the pages from this book and cutting the question cards apart. (If you prefer to keep the book intact, simply photocopy the question cards from the section or sections you wish to use.) For added durability, laminate the pages before you cut the cards apart. To help you identify topic categories, a different border has been used for each of the ten sections of the book.

Make a bulletin board display using the headers provided on pages 6 and 7. Divide the headers with colored yarn. Select five categories at a time (or more, if you prefer) and pin five question cards from the five categories under each heading. Attach an unlined index card with a dollar value written on it over each question card. The more difficult questions should be worth more money and should be placed farther down on the quiz board.

Once the quiz board is set up, it can be used over and over by simply changing the category headers and/or replacing question cards with new ones.

Students can get together and decide on the game rules as a class. Encourage them to think of other topics that relate to social studies and to add their own question cards to the board. A moderator can be selected, and someone can be assigned to check to see if the questions have been answered correctly by simply looking on the reverse side of the question cards on the board.

Select a scorekeeper to keep track of money earned. You can also use play money as Quiz Whiz bucks to award players. Play money can be found at many school supply and toy stores.

Triple Tic-Tac-Toe

This is a great game for students to play at a social studies center when they've completed their class assignments. Reproduce copies of the Triple Tic-Tac-Toe game board on page 8, and place them at the center along with the question cards. Students may play with partners, taking turns drawing questions from the pile and answering them. If a player answers a question correctly, he or she marks an X or an O in pencil on any one of the three Tic-Tac-Toe grids. Students must play defensively, trying to block their opponents from getting three correct answers in a row in any direction while attempting to score Tic-Tac-Toe themselves.

Quiz Whiz Social Studies Bee

Use questions for a Quiz Whiz Social Studies Bee, organized like a spelling bee. Contestants are eliminated as they miss questions asked by a student moderator. Have class champs challenge each other, or organize a school-wide Quiz Whiz Social Studies Bee.

Radio or Television Game Show

Use Quiz Whiz questions to organize a classroom quiz show in a radio or television format. Select one student to be the "host" and four to six students to be "contestants." Create your own rules: correct answers can earn Quiz Whiz bucks; incorrect answers might lose bucks. The end of the game can come after a predetermined period of time, or after a certain number of questions have been asked and answered.

Quiz Whiz Question of the Day

Select some of the most difficult questions and use them as research challenges for a class assignment each day. Students can work alone or with partners to answer the question of the day. This is also a good way to get students to seek information on the Internet. Award Quiz Whiz bucks to the first student(s) to find the correct answer. Quiz Whiz bucks can be redeemed for awards at the end of the week. A variation would be to select a difficult question each day for homework or for an extra-credit challenge.

Cities & States

Famous Men & Women

Government

History

Landmarks, Symbols, & Famous Places

North, South, East, & West

Presidents
of the **United States**

State Capitals

U.S. Geography

World Geography

Triple Tic-Tac-Toe Game Board

SOCIAL STUDIES
Quiz Whiz

The cities of Columbus, Akron, and Cincinnati are found in which state?

SOCIAL STUDIES
Quiz Whiz

How many states have the word "South" in their names?

SOCIAL STUDIES
Quiz Whiz

The cities of Billings, Great Falls, Butte, and Helena are found in which state?

SOCIAL STUDIES
Quiz Whiz

In 1787, which was the first state to enter the Union?

SOCIAL STUDIES
Quiz Whiz

The cities of Macon, Atlanta, and Savannah are found in which state?

SOCIAL STUDIES
Quiz Whiz

Which was the last state admitted to the Union?

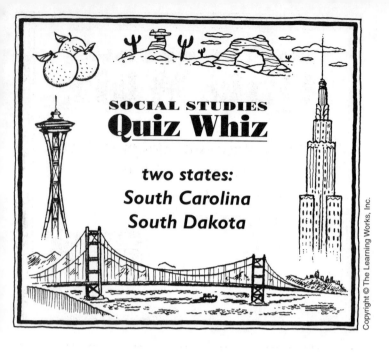

SOCIAL STUDIES
Quiz Whiz

two states:
South Carolina
South Dakota

SOCIAL STUDIES
Quiz Whiz

Ohio

SOCIAL STUDIES
Quiz Whiz

Delaware

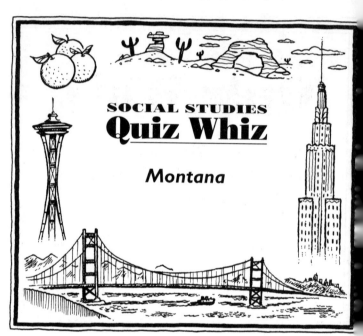

SOCIAL STUDIES
Quiz Whiz

Montana

SOCIAL STUDIES
Quiz Whiz

Hawaii

SOCIAL STUDIES
Quiz Whiz

Georgia

SOCIAL STUDIES
Quiz Whiz

The cities of Santa Fe, Carlsbad, and Albuquerque are found in which state?

SOCIAL STUDIES
Quiz Whiz

Which state is nicknamed the Sunshine State and has the orange blossom as its state flower?

SOCIAL STUDIES
Quiz Whiz

The cities of Birmingham, Huntsville, and Montgomery are found in which state?

SOCIAL STUDIES
Quiz Whiz

Which state has the longest coastline in the United States?

SOCIAL STUDIES
Quiz Whiz

How many states have the word "North" in their names?

SOCIAL STUDIES
Quiz Whiz

The cities of Bismarck, Fargo, and Grand Forks are found in which state?

SOCIAL STUDIES
Quiz Whiz

Florida

SOCIAL STUDIES
Quiz Whiz

New Mexico

SOCIAL STUDIES
Quiz Whiz

Alaska

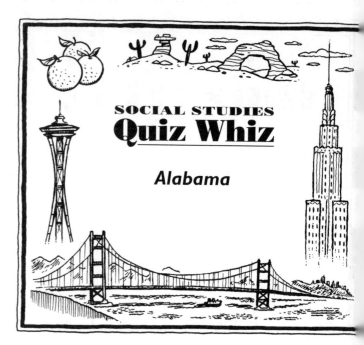

SOCIAL STUDIES
Quiz Whiz

Alabama

SOCIAL STUDIES
Quiz Whiz

North Dakota

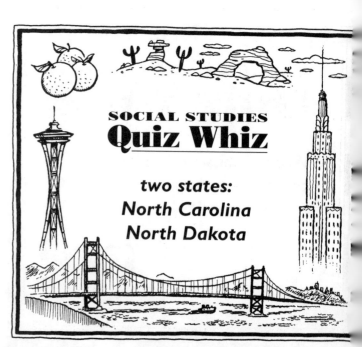

SOCIAL STUDIES
Quiz Whiz

two states:
North Carolina
North Dakota

SOCIAL STUDIES
Quiz Whiz

Which three states border California?

SOCIAL STUDIES
Quiz Whiz

The cities of Amarillo, San Antonio, and Houston are found in which state?

SOCIAL STUDIES
Quiz Whiz

Which state is nicknamed "The Land of Enchantment"?

SOCIAL STUDIES
Quiz Whiz

The cities of Fort Wayne, Gary, and Indianapolis are found in which state?

SOCIAL STUDIES
Quiz Whiz

Which is the only state completely surrounded by water?

SOCIAL STUDIES
Quiz Whiz

The cities of Tampa, Orlando, and St. Petersburg are found in which state?

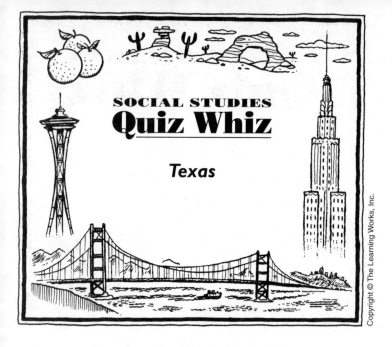

SOCIAL STUDIES
Quiz Whiz
Texas

SOCIAL STUDIES
Quiz Whiz
Arizona, Nevada, and Oregon

SOCIAL STUDIES
Quiz Whiz
Indiana

SOCIAL STUDIES
Quiz Whiz
New Mexico

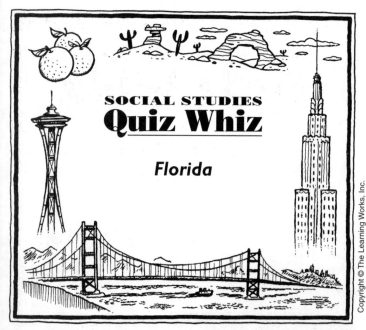

SOCIAL STUDIES
Quiz Whiz
Florida

SOCIAL STUDIES
Quiz Whiz
Hawaii

SOCIAL STUDIES
Quiz Whiz

Which western state contains the Great Salt Lake?

SOCIAL STUDIES
Quiz Whiz

The cities of Spokane, Tacoma, and Seattle are found in which state?

SOCIAL STUDIES
Quiz Whiz

Which is the smallest in size of the fifty states?

SOCIAL STUDIES
Quiz Whiz

Long Island is part of which state?

SOCIAL STUDIES
Quiz Whiz

The cities of Topeka, Wichita, and Parsons are found in which state?

SOCIAL STUDIES
Quiz Whiz

Which state is nicknamed "The Bluegrass State"?

SOCIAL STUDIES
Quiz Whiz

Washington

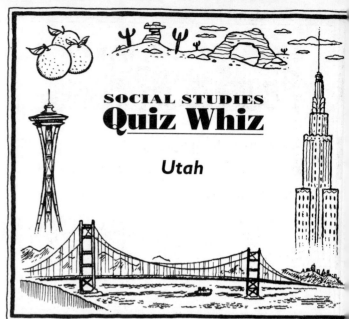

SOCIAL STUDIES
Quiz Whiz

Utah

SOCIAL STUDIES
Quiz Whiz

New York

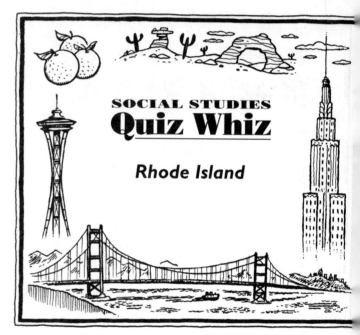

SOCIAL STUDIES
Quiz Whiz

Rhode Island

SOCIAL STUDIES
Quiz Whiz

Kentucky

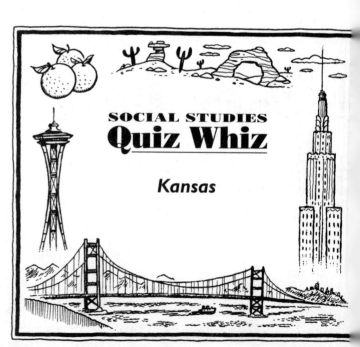

SOCIAL STUDIES
Quiz Whiz

Kansas

SOCIAL STUDIES
Quiz Whiz

Sequoia–Kings Canyon National Park is located in which state?

SOCIAL STUDIES
Quiz Whiz

The cities of Reno, Carson City, and Las Vegas are found in which state?

SOCIAL STUDIES
Quiz Whiz

Which Atlantic state is home to Cape Lookout and Cape Hatteras?

SOCIAL STUDIES
Quiz Whiz

Aberdeen, Sioux Falls, and Webster are cities found in which state?

SOCIAL STUDIES
Quiz Whiz

The cities of Denver, Pueblo, and Vail are found in which state?

SOCIAL STUDIES
Quiz Whiz

The Rio Grande flows from north to south through which western state, dividing it in half?

SOCIAL STUDIES
Quiz Whiz

Nevada

SOCIAL STUDIES
Quiz Whiz

California

SOCIAL STUDIES
Quiz Whiz

South Dakota

SOCIAL STUDIES
Quiz Whiz

North Carolina

SOCIAL STUDIES
Quiz Whiz

New Mexico

SOCIAL STUDIES
Quiz Whiz

Colorado

Copyright © The Learning Works, Inc.

Copyright © The Learning Works, Inc.

Copyright © The Learning Works, Inc.

SOCIAL STUDIES Quiz Whiz

Salem, Portland, and Eugene are cities found in which state?

SOCIAL STUDIES Quiz Whiz

Which state straddles Chesapeake Bay?

SOCIAL STUDIES Quiz Whiz

The cities of Chattanooga, Memphis, and Nashville are found in which state?

SOCIAL STUDIES Quiz Whiz

Which state lies along both Lake Ontario and Lake Erie?

SOCIAL STUDIES Quiz Whiz

Grand Rapids, Flint, and Detroit are cities found in which state?

SOCIAL STUDIES Quiz Whiz

Bridgeport, Hartford, and New Haven are cities found in which state?

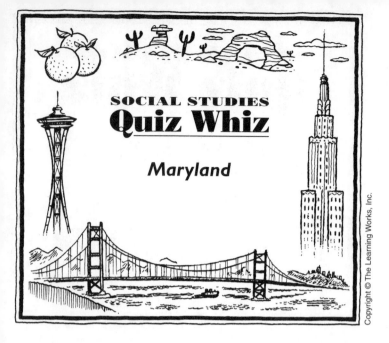

SOCIAL STUDIES
Quiz Whiz

Maryland

SOCIAL STUDIES
Quiz Whiz

Oregon

SOCIAL STUDIES
Quiz Whiz

New York

SOCIAL STUDIES
Quiz Whiz

Tennessee

SOCIAL STUDIES
Quiz Whiz

Connecticut

SOCIAL STUDIES
Quiz Whiz

Michigan

SOCIAL STUDIES
Quiz Whiz

What nickname was given to legendary baseball player George Herman Ruth?

SOCIAL STUDIES
Quiz Whiz

Who was the first navigator to explore the coast of California?

SOCIAL STUDIES
Quiz Whiz

Which native American woman was a guide for Lewis and Clark when they explored the Louisiana Purchase?

SOCIAL STUDIES
Quiz Whiz

Who was the Spanish explorer who first sighted the Pacific Ocean and named it the Great South Sea?

SOCIAL STUDIES
Quiz Whiz

Who invented the telegraph?

SOCIAL STUDIES
Quiz Whiz

Which African-American woman refused to give up her seat on a bus in Montgomery, Alabama, in 1955?

SOCIAL STUDIES
Quiz Whiz

Juan Rodríguez Cabrillo

SOCIAL STUDIES
Quiz Whiz

Babe

SOCIAL STUDIES
Quiz Whiz

Vasco Núñez de Balboa

SOCIAL STUDIES
Quiz Whiz

Sacagawea

SOCIAL STUDIES
Quiz Whiz

Rosa Parks

SOCIAL STUDIES
Quiz Whiz

Samuel F.B. Morse

SOCIAL STUDIES
Quiz Whiz

Which Portugese explorer sailed around the tip of Africa and across the Indian Ocean to India?

SOCIAL STUDIES
Quiz Whiz

Who is credited with making the first American flag?

SOCIAL STUDIES
Quiz Whiz

Who was the Viking who discovered Greenland?

SOCIAL STUDIES
Quiz Whiz

For whom was the state of Pennsylvania named?

SOCIAL STUDIES
Quiz Whiz

Who was the first woman to fly solo across the Atlantic?

SOCIAL STUDIES
Quiz Whiz

Who was the English explorer who sailed to North America in a ship called the Half Moon?

SOCIAL STUDIES
Quiz Whiz

Betsy Ross

SOCIAL STUDIES
Quiz Whiz

Vasco da Gama

SOCIAL STUDIES
Quiz Whiz

William Penn

SOCIAL STUDIES
Quiz Whiz

Leif Ericson

SOCIAL STUDIES
Quiz Whiz

Henry Hudson

SOCIAL STUDIES
Quiz Whiz

Amelia Earhart

SOCIAL STUDIES
Quiz Whiz

What did Captain James Cook call the Hawaiian Islands in 1778?

SOCIAL STUDIES
Quiz Whiz

Who was the explorer who sailed down the coast of South America and discovered Peru?

SOCIAL STUDIES
Quiz Whiz

What famous artist painted the Mona Lisa?

SOCIAL STUDIES
Quiz Whiz

Who was the founder of the colony of Rhode Island?

SOCIAL STUDIES
Quiz Whiz

Which Spanish explorer searched the southwestern United States in search of the "Seven Cities of Cíbola"?

SOCIAL STUDIES
Quiz Whiz

What African-American led the bus boycott in Montgomery, Alabama?

SOCIAL STUDIES
Quiz Whiz

Francisco Pizarro

SOCIAL STUDIES
Quiz Whiz

the Sandwich Islands

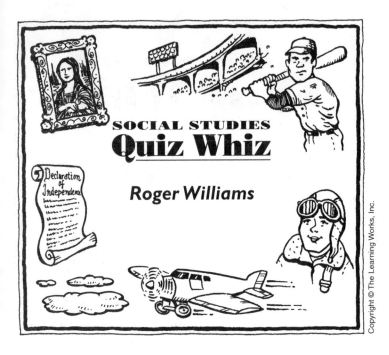

SOCIAL STUDIES
Quiz Whiz

Roger Williams

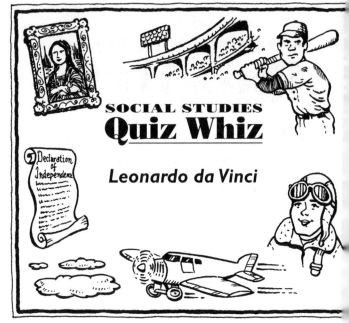

SOCIAL STUDIES
Quiz Whiz

Leonardo da Vinci

SOCIAL STUDIES
Quiz Whiz

Martin Luther King, Jr.

SOCIAL STUDIES
Quiz Whiz

Francisco Vásquez
de Coronado

SOCIAL STUDIES
Quiz Whiz

Which Spanish explorer
conquered the Aztecs
of Mexico?

SOCIAL STUDIES
Quiz Whiz

Who made the first solo
nonstop flight across the
Atlantic in the Spirit
of St. Louis?

SOCIAL STUDIES
Quiz Whiz

What famous composer kept
writing music even after
he went deaf?

SOCIAL STUDIES
Quiz Whiz

Who served as vice president
under George W. Bush?

SOCIAL STUDIES
Quiz Whiz

Who was the Spanish
explorer who searched
Florida for the "fountain
of youth"?

SOCIAL STUDIES
Quiz Whiz

Who was the first astronaut
to walk on the moon?

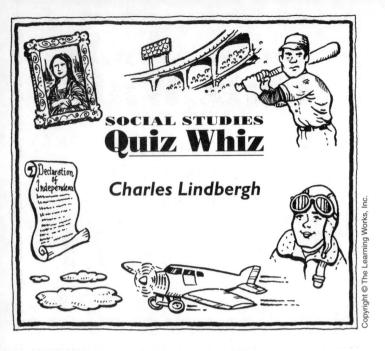

SOCIAL STUDIES
Quiz Whiz

Charles Lindbergh

SOCIAL STUDIES
Quiz Whiz

Hernando Cortes

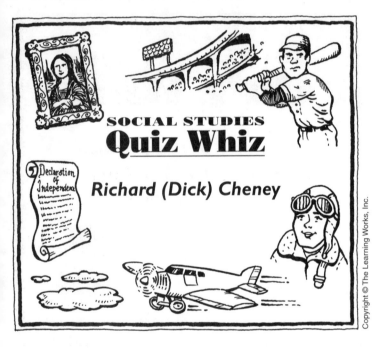

SOCIAL STUDIES
Quiz Whiz

Richard (Dick) Cheney

SOCIAL STUDIES
Quiz Whiz

Ludwig van Beethoven

SOCIAL STUDIES
Quiz Whiz

Neil Armstrong

SOCIAL STUDIES
Quiz Whiz

Ponce de León

SOCIAL STUDIES
Quiz Whiz

What Italian painter, sculptor, and architect sculpted David and painted the ceiling of the Sistine Chapel?

SOCIAL STUDIES
Quiz Whiz

Who was the general in command of the Confederate forces during the Civil War?

SOCIAL STUDIES
Quiz Whiz

Who was the first person to sign the Declaration of Independence as president of the Continental Congress?

SOCIAL STUDIES
Quiz Whiz

What brothers flew the first successful airplane in Kitty Hawk, North Carolina?

SOCIAL STUDIES
Quiz Whiz

Who was the first American woman to travel in space?

SOCIAL STUDIES
Quiz Whiz

Who served as secretary of defense when George W. Bush was president?

SOCIAL STUDIES
Quiz Whiz

Robert E. Lee

SOCIAL STUDIES
Quiz Whiz

Michelangelo

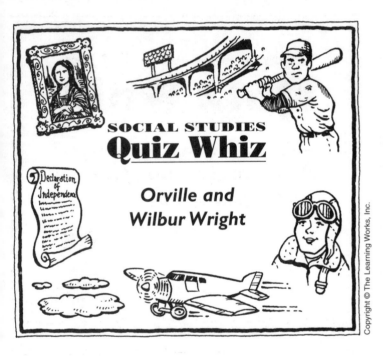

SOCIAL STUDIES
Quiz Whiz

Orville and Wilbur Wright

SOCIAL STUDIES
Quiz Whiz

John Hancock

SOCIAL STUDIES
Quiz Whiz

Donald Rumsfeld

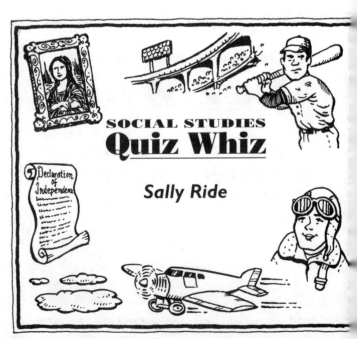

SOCIAL STUDIES
Quiz Whiz

Sally Ride

SOCIAL STUDIES
Quiz Whiz

What French navigator and explorer founded the city of Quebec in Canada?

SOCIAL STUDIES
Quiz Whiz

Who was the Dutch colonial official who purchased Manhattan Island from the native Americans?

SOCIAL STUDIES
Quiz Whiz

Who was the first woman to be appointed a justice of the United States Supreme Court?

SOCIAL STUDIES
Quiz Whiz

Who was the first African-American chairman of the Joint Chiefs of Staff?

SOCIAL STUDIES
Quiz Whiz

Which general commanded the Union Army during the Civil War?

SOCIAL STUDIES
Quiz Whiz

Who was the first American in space?

SOCIAL STUDIES
Quiz Whiz
Peter Minuit

SOCIAL STUDIES
Quiz Whiz
Samuel de Champlain

SOCIAL STUDIES
Quiz Whiz
Colin Powell

SOCIAL STUDIES
Quiz Whiz
Sandra Day O'Connor

SOCIAL STUDIES
Quiz Whiz
Alan Shepard, Jr.

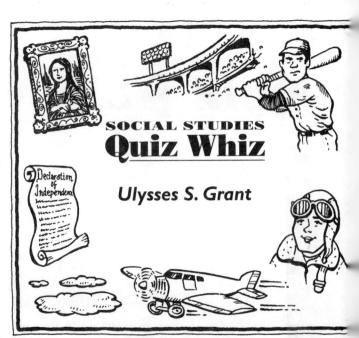

SOCIAL STUDIES
Quiz Whiz
Ulysses S. Grant

SOCIAL STUDIES
Quiz Whiz

What important document, known as "the supreme law of the land," was written in 1787 at a convention in Philadelphia?

SOCIAL STUDIES
Quiz Whiz

The president, the cabinet, and various executive agencies make up which branch of government?

SOCIAL STUDIES
Quiz Whiz

What is a proposal called that is presented to a legislative body for possible enactment as a law?

SOCIAL STUDIES
Quiz Whiz

How many justices serve on the United States Supreme Court?

SOCIAL STUDIES
Quiz Whiz

What does the acronym NATO stand for?

SOCIAL STUDIES
Quiz Whiz

What is another name for the first ten amendments to the United States Constitution?

SOCIAL STUDIES
Quiz Whiz

the executive branch

SOCIAL STUDIES
Quiz Whiz

the Constitution

SOCIAL STUDIES
Quiz Whiz

nine justices

SOCIAL STUDIES
Quiz Whiz

a bill

SOCIAL STUDIES
Quiz Whiz

the Bill of Rights

SOCIAL STUDIES
Quiz Whiz

North Atlantic Treaty Organization

SOCIAL STUDIES
Quiz Whiz

The Senate of the United States is made up of how many senators from each state?

SOCIAL STUDIES
Quiz Whiz

What is an addition or change to the U.S. Constitution called?

SOCIAL STUDIES
Quiz Whiz

Which elected official acts as commander-in-chief of the armed forces?

SOCIAL STUDIES
Quiz Whiz

What animal is the symbol of the Republican Party?

SOCIAL STUDIES
Quiz Whiz

The number of representatives that each state sends to the House of Representatives is based on what?

SOCIAL STUDIES
Quiz Whiz

The Supreme Court and other federal courts make up which branch of government?

SOCIAL STUDIES
Quiz Whiz

an amendment

SOCIAL STUDIES
Quiz Whiz

two senators

SOCIAL STUDIES
Quiz Whiz

the elephant

SOCIAL STUDIES
Quiz Whiz

the president

SOCIAL STUDIES
Quiz Whiz

the judicial branch

SOCIAL STUDIES
Quiz Whiz

population

SOCIAL STUDIES
Quiz Whiz

In order to be elected to the House of Representatives, a person must be a U.S. citizen for at least how many years?

SOCIAL STUDIES
Quiz Whiz

What are the names of the two major political parties in the United States?

SOCIAL STUDIES
Quiz Whiz

What does the acronym FBI stand for?

SOCIAL STUDIES
Quiz Whiz

Which amendment to the United States Constitution guaranteed women the right to vote?

SOCIAL STUDIES
Quiz Whiz

Which branch of the U.S. government enacts laws?

SOCIAL STUDIES
Quiz Whiz

How many presidential advisers make up the cabinet?

SOCIAL STUDIES
Quiz Whiz

the Democrats and
the Republicans

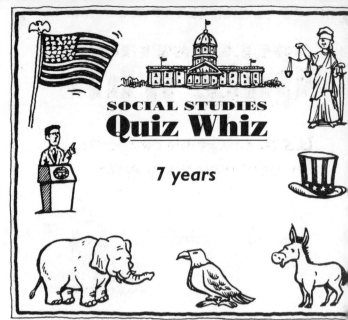

SOCIAL STUDIES
Quiz Whiz

7 years

SOCIAL STUDIES
Quiz Whiz

the 19th
Amendment

SOCIAL STUDIES
Quiz Whiz

Federal Bureau
of Investigation

SOCIAL STUDIES
Quiz Whiz

14 advisers

SOCIAL STUDIES
Quiz Whiz

the legislative branch

SOCIAL STUDIES
Quiz Whiz

U.S. Senators are elected to serve for how many years?

SOCIAL STUDIES
Quiz Whiz

What five-sided building in Virginia serves as the headquarters of the Department of Defense?

SOCIAL STUDIES
Quiz Whiz

What is the minimum age a person must be in order to be president of the United States?

SOCIAL STUDIES
Quiz Whiz

What animal is the symbol of the Democratic Party?

SOCIAL STUDIES
Quiz Whiz

What is the system called that prevents one branch of the government from having too much power over another?

SOCIAL STUDIES
Quiz Whiz

Which branch of government interprets the law?

SOCIAL STUDIES
Quiz Whiz

the Pentagon

SOCIAL STUDIES
Quiz Whiz

6 years

SOCIAL STUDIES
Quiz Whiz

the donkey

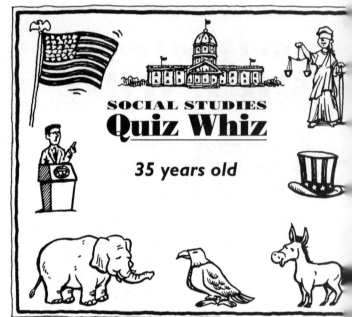

SOCIAL STUDIES
Quiz Whiz

35 years old

SOCIAL STUDIES
Quiz Whiz

the judicial branch

SOCIAL STUDIES
Quiz Whiz

checks and balances

SOCIAL STUDIES
Quiz Whiz

A bill can become a law despite a presidential veto if both the Senate and the House pass the bill by what majority?

SOCIAL STUDIES
Quiz Whiz

In order to be a senator, a person must be a citizen of the U.S. for a minimum of how many years?

SOCIAL STUDIES
Quiz Whiz

In an election, what is the device called by which a voter registers his or her choice?

SOCIAL STUDIES
Quiz Whiz

How many amendments have been made to the Constitution of the United States?

SOCIAL STUDIES
Quiz Whiz

What does the acronym CIA stand for?

SOCIAL STUDIES
Quiz Whiz

Who becomes president if both the president and vice president of the United States are unable to serve?

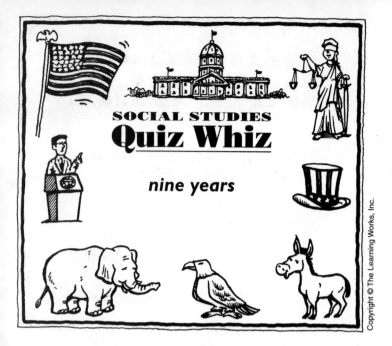

SOCIAL STUDIES
Quiz Whiz

nine years

SOCIAL STUDIES
Quiz Whiz

two-thirds

SOCIAL STUDIES
Quiz Whiz

27 amendments

SOCIAL STUDIES
Quiz Whiz

a ballot

SOCIAL STUDIES
Quiz Whiz

*the Speaker
of the House
of Representatives*

SOCIAL STUDIES
Quiz Whiz

*Central Intelligence
Agency*

SOCIAL STUDIES
Quiz Whiz

What is a state election called in which delegates to the nominating convention are chosen?

SOCIAL STUDIES
Quiz Whiz

What is the highest court in the United States?

SOCIAL STUDIES
Quiz Whiz

What kind of law deals with disputes between individuals?

SOCIAL STUDIES
Quiz Whiz

What is the minimum age a citizen of the U.S. must be in order to vote in a state or federal election?

SOCIAL STUDIES
Quiz Whiz

Which of the following is a state government not authorized to do: issue licenses, print money, conduct elections, or regulate intrastate commerce?

SOCIAL STUDIES
Quiz Whiz

How many United States senators are there?

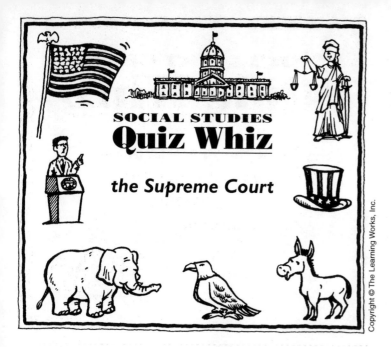

SOCIAL STUDIES
Quiz Whiz

the Supreme Court

SOCIAL STUDIES
Quiz Whiz

primary

SOCIAL STUDIES
Quiz Whiz

18 years old

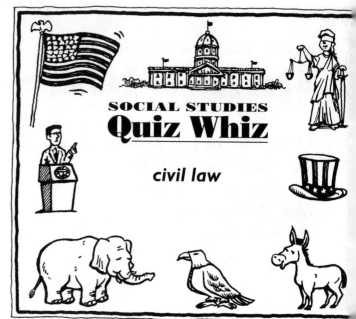

SOCIAL STUDIES
Quiz Whiz

civil law

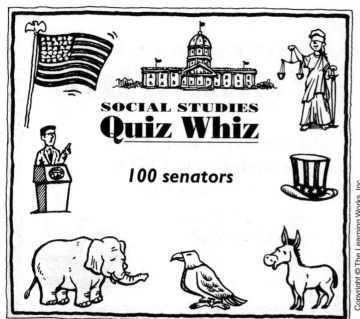

SOCIAL STUDIES
Quiz Whiz

100 senators

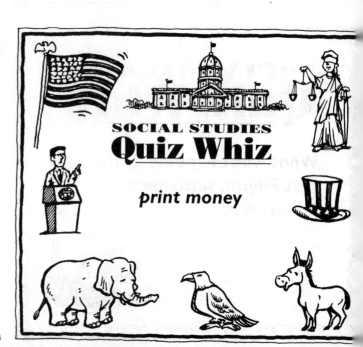

SOCIAL STUDIES
Quiz Whiz

print money

SOCIAL STUDIES
Quiz Whiz

For whom was America named?

SOCIAL STUDIES
Quiz Whiz

What was the name of the document by which the first U.S. government was established?

SOCIAL STUDIES
Quiz Whiz

What war was fought between the north and the south from 1861 to 1865, over the issues of slavery and states' rights?

SOCIAL STUDIES
Quiz Whiz

What was the name of the first permanent English settlement in America, founded in 1607?

SOCIAL STUDIES
Quiz Whiz

What was the name of the first Pilgrim settlement in America?

SOCIAL STUDIES
Quiz Whiz

What battle fought in Pennsylvania in 1863 is often considered the turning point of the Civil War?

SOCIAL STUDIES
Quiz Whiz

the Articles of Confederation

SOCIAL STUDIES
Quiz Whiz

Amerigo Vespucci

SOCIAL STUDIES
Quiz Whiz

Jamestown

SOCIAL STUDIES
Quiz Whiz

the Civil War

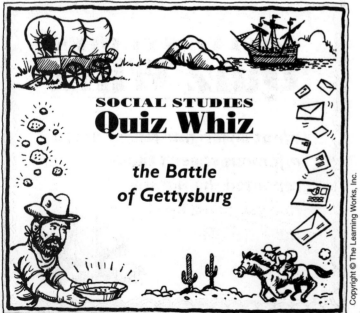

SOCIAL STUDIES
Quiz Whiz

the Battle of Gettysburg

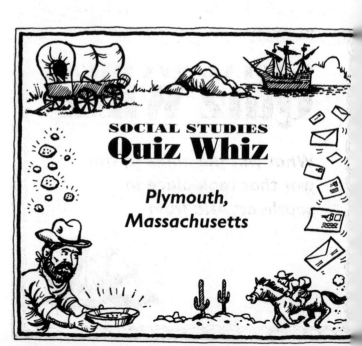

SOCIAL STUDIES
Quiz Whiz

Plymouth, Massachusetts

SOCIAL STUDIES
Quiz Whiz

The War of 1812 was fought between the United States and which country?

SOCIAL STUDIES
Quiz Whiz

Which of the following did an "abolitionist" want to do away with: taxes, slavery, alcohol, or government?

SOCIAL STUDIES
Quiz Whiz

What product did angry American colonists toss into the Boston harbor in 1773 in protest of taxes imposed by the British?

SOCIAL STUDIES
Quiz Whiz

During the American Revolution, where was the winter headquarters of George Washington?

SOCIAL STUDIES
Quiz Whiz

What was the name of the war that took place in southeast Asia from 1957 to 1975?

SOCIAL STUDIES
Quiz Whiz

What civil rights leader made a famous speech that repeated the phrase, "I have a dream"?

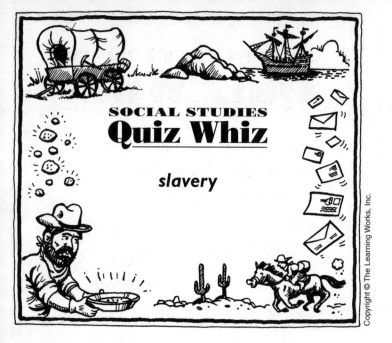

SOCIAL STUDIES
Quiz Whiz

slavery

SOCIAL STUDIES
Quiz Whiz

Great Britain

SOCIAL STUDIES
Quiz Whiz

Valley Forge, Pennsylvania

SOCIAL STUDIES
Quiz Whiz

tea

SOCIAL STUDIES
Quiz Whiz

Martin Luther King, Jr.

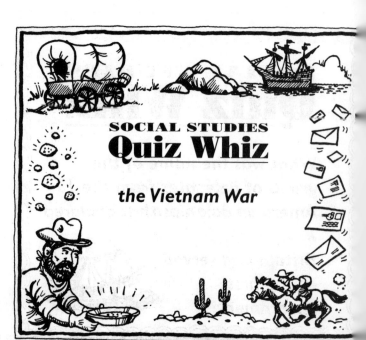

SOCIAL STUDIES
Quiz Whiz

the Vietnam War

SOCIAL STUDIES
Quiz Whiz

What was a person called who came to California in 1849 in search of gold?

SOCIAL STUDIES
Quiz Whiz

The United States fought against which country in the Persian Gulf War?

SOCIAL STUDIES
Quiz Whiz

"The British are coming! The British are coming!" was the cry of which colonial American patriot?

SOCIAL STUDIES
Quiz Whiz

What was the name of the queen of Spain who sponsored the voyages of Christopher Columbus?

SOCIAL STUDIES
Quiz Whiz

What was the name of the group of delegates from the 13 American colonies that declared independence from Britain and served as the first government?

SOCIAL STUDIES
Quiz Whiz

Who said, "Give me liberty, or give me death!"?

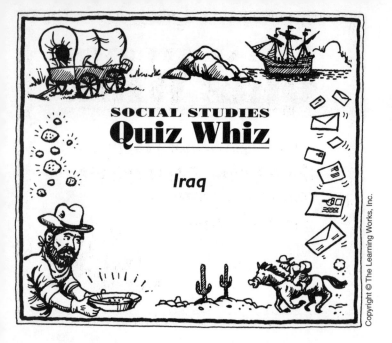

SOCIAL STUDIES
Quiz Whiz

Iraq

SOCIAL STUDIES
Quiz Whiz

forty-niner

SOCIAL STUDIES
Quiz Whiz

Queen Isabella

SOCIAL STUDIES
Quiz Whiz

Paul Revere

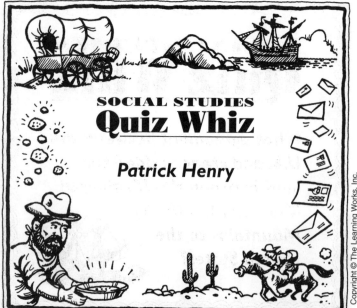

SOCIAL STUDIES
Quiz Whiz

Patrick Henry

SOCIAL STUDIES
Quiz Whiz

the Continental Congress

SOCIAL STUDIES
Quiz Whiz

What was an American colonist called who supported the movement for independence?

SOCIAL STUDIES
Quiz Whiz

Which amendment to the U.S. Constitution gave citizens the right to "a speedy and public trial"?

SOCIAL STUDIES
Quiz Whiz

Who was the president of the Confederacy during the Civil War?

SOCIAL STUDIES
Quiz Whiz

What important document was signed on July 4, 1776?

SOCIAL STUDIES
Quiz Whiz

What is a person called who leaves his or her own country to live permanently in another country?

SOCIAL STUDIES
Quiz Whiz

What agreement between the U.S. and France added the land between the Mississippi River and the Rocky Mountains to the United States?

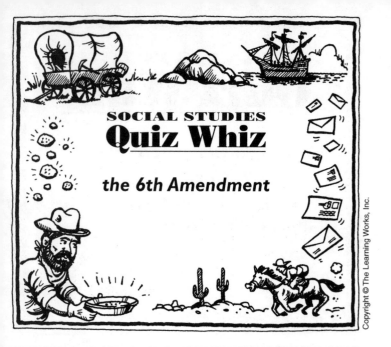

SOCIAL STUDIES
Quiz Whiz

the 6th Amendment

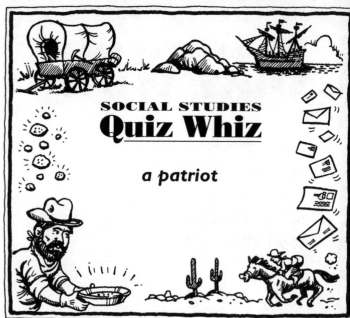

SOCIAL STUDIES
Quiz Whiz

a patriot

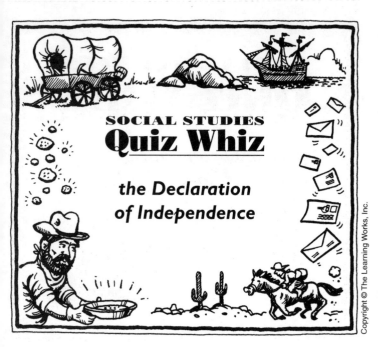

SOCIAL STUDIES
Quiz Whiz

the Declaration of Independence

SOCIAL STUDIES
Quiz Whiz

Jefferson Davis

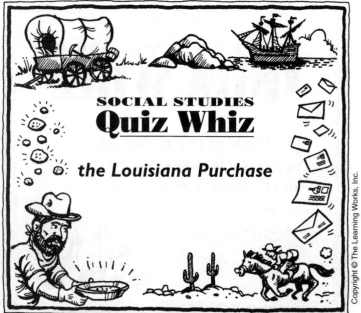

SOCIAL STUDIES
Quiz Whiz

the Louisiana Purchase

SOCIAL STUDIES
Quiz Whiz

an immigrant

SOCIAL STUDIES
Quiz Whiz

On September 11, 2001, terrorists struck the World Trade Center in New York and what building in Washington, D.C.?

SOCIAL STUDIES
Quiz Whiz

What was the overland mail service called that ran between Missouri and California in 1860 and 1861?

SOCIAL STUDIES
Quiz Whiz

What agreement between the men aboard the Mayflower set up a consensual government for the Plymouth colony?

SOCIAL STUDIES
Quiz Whiz

The battle of Lexington and Concord in 1775 was the beginning of which war?

SOCIAL STUDIES
Quiz Whiz

On December 7, 1941, which country attacked the U.S. fleet at Pearl Harbor in Hawaii?

SOCIAL STUDIES
Quiz Whiz

In which of the following years did World War II begin: 1939, 1949, 1959, or 1969?

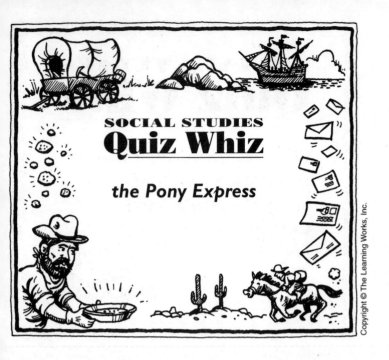

SOCIAL STUDIES
Quiz Whiz

the Pony Express

SOCIAL STUDIES
Quiz Whiz

the Pentagon

SOCIAL STUDIES
Quiz Whiz

*the American
Revolution*

SOCIAL STUDIES
Quiz Whiz

*the Mayflower
Compact*

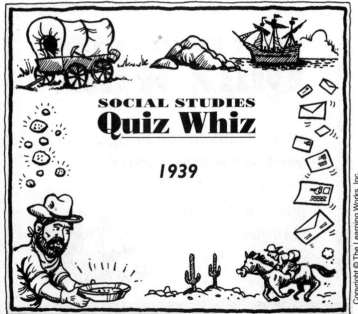

SOCIAL STUDIES
Quiz Whiz

1939

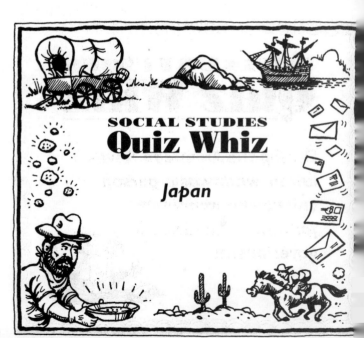

SOCIAL STUDIES
Quiz Whiz

Japan

SOCIAL STUDIES
Quiz Whiz

In which city was President John F. Kennedy assassinated?

SOCIAL STUDIES
Quiz Whiz

What terrorist leader was the focus of attacks by U.S. forces in Afghanistan in 2001?

SOCIAL STUDIES
Quiz Whiz

What was the name of the prime minister who led Britain during World War II?

SOCIAL STUDIES
Quiz Whiz

What famous trail that went from Independence, Missouri, to the west coast was an important route for settlers in the 1840s?

SOCIAL STUDIES
Quiz Whiz

During the American Revolution, what was a person called who remained faithful to the British government?

SOCIAL STUDIES
Quiz Whiz

What "vehicle" of escape was used by southern slaves fleeing to northern free states and Canada?

SOCIAL STUDIES
Quiz Whiz

Osama bin Laden

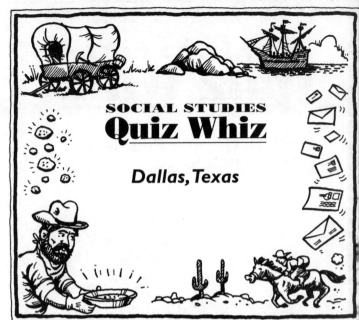

SOCIAL STUDIES
Quiz Whiz

Dallas, Texas

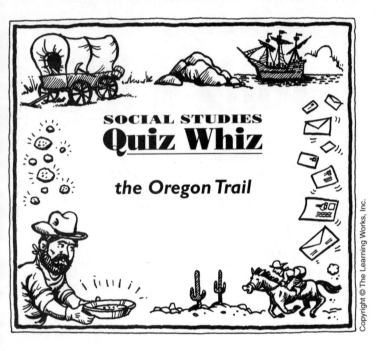

SOCIAL STUDIES
Quiz Whiz

the Oregon Trail

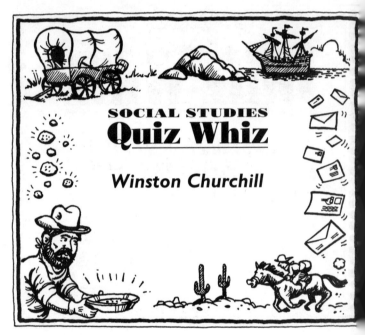

SOCIAL STUDIES
Quiz Whiz

Winston Churchill

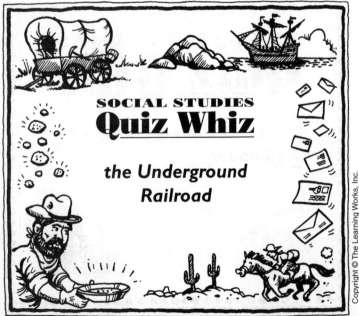

SOCIAL STUDIES
Quiz Whiz

the Underground Railroad

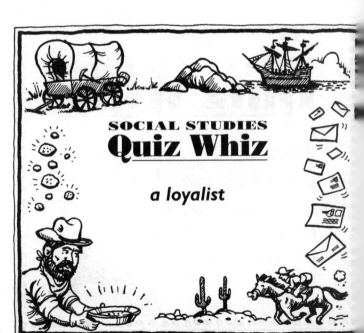

SOCIAL STUDIES
Quiz Whiz

a loyalist

SOCIAL STUDIES
Quiz Whiz

In what city was the U.S. Constitution written?

SOCIAL STUDIES
Quiz Whiz

Carlsbad Caverns National Park, home of the world's largest caves, is located in which state?

SOCIAL STUDIES
Quiz Whiz

In which city and state is the Baseball Hall of Fame and Museum located?

SOCIAL STUDIES
Quiz Whiz

The Declaration of Independence was signed in what building in Philadelphia in 1776?

SOCIAL STUDIES
Quiz Whiz

What city in France is home to the Eiffel Tower?

SOCIAL STUDIES
Quiz Whiz

What is the largest province in Canada?

SOCIAL STUDIES
Quiz Whiz

New Mexico

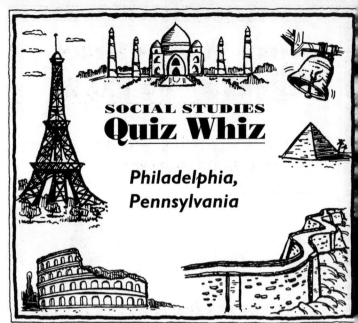

SOCIAL STUDIES
Quiz Whiz

Philadelphia,
Pennsylvania

SOCIAL STUDIES
Quiz Whiz

Independence Hall

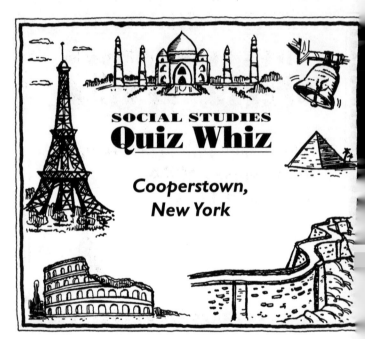

SOCIAL STUDIES
Quiz Whiz

Cooperstown,
New York

SOCIAL STUDIES
Quiz Whiz

Quebec

SOCIAL STUDIES
Quiz Whiz

Paris

SOCIAL STUDIES
Quiz Whiz

In what city is the United Nations headquarters located?

SOCIAL STUDIES
Quiz Whiz

In what city is the original Liberty Bell located?

SOCIAL STUDIES
Quiz Whiz

What is the official home of the president of the United States?

SOCIAL STUDIES
Quiz Whiz

What is the largest concrete dam in the United States, located near Spokane, Washington?

SOCIAL STUDIES
Quiz Whiz

What landmark in San Antonio, Texas, was the site of a famous battle for Texan independence?

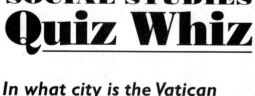

SOCIAL STUDIES
Quiz Whiz

In what city is the Vatican located?

SOCIAL STUDIES
Quiz Whiz

*Philadelphia,
Pennsylvania*

SOCIAL STUDIES
Quiz Whiz

New York, New York

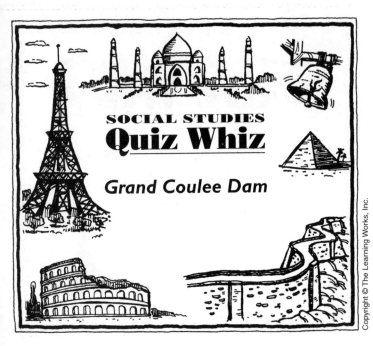

SOCIAL STUDIES
Quiz Whiz

Grand Coulee Dam

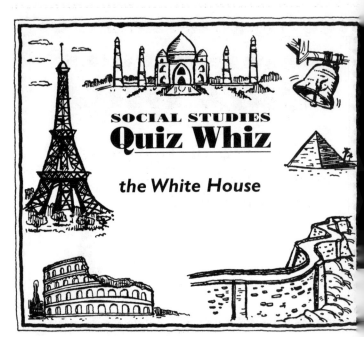

SOCIAL STUDIES
Quiz Whiz

the White House

SOCIAL STUDIES
Quiz Whiz

*Vatican City
in Rome*

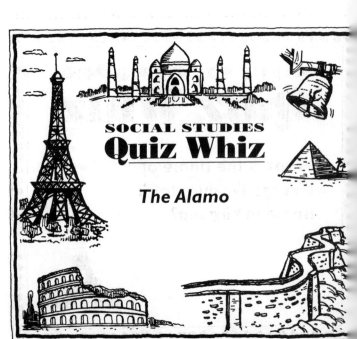

SOCIAL STUDIES
Quiz Whiz

The Alamo

SOCIAL STUDIES
Quiz Whiz

What street in New York City is the financial capital of the United States?

SOCIAL STUDIES
Quiz Whiz

In what state is Glacier National Park located?

SOCIAL STUDIES
Quiz Whiz

What city in Italy is home to a bell tower called the "Leaning Tower"?

SOCIAL STUDIES
Quiz Whiz

In what domed building in Washington, D.C., does the Congress meet?

SOCIAL STUDIES
Quiz Whiz

What is the name of George Washington's home in Virginia?

SOCIAL STUDIES
Quiz Whiz

What is the world's tallest skyscraper?

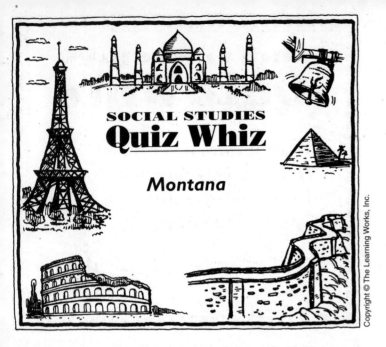

SOCIAL STUDIES
Quiz Whiz

Montana

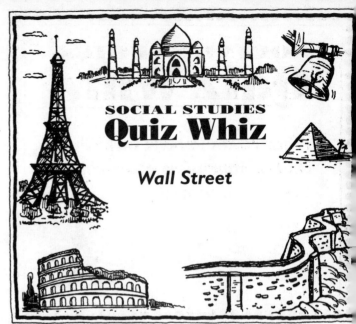

SOCIAL STUDIES
Quiz Whiz

Wall Street

SOCIAL STUDIES
Quiz Whiz

the Capitol

SOCIAL STUDIES
Quiz Whiz

Pisa

SOCIAL STUDIES
Quiz Whiz

Sears Tower,
Chicago

SOCIAL STUDIES
Quiz Whiz

Mount Vernon

SOCIAL STUDIES
Quiz Whiz

What do the stripes on the United States flag represent?

SOCIAL STUDIES
Quiz Whiz

What is the name of the theater where Abraham Lincoln was assassinated by John Wilkes Booth?

SOCIAL STUDIES
Quiz Whiz

What is the name of the world's largest museum complex, located in Washington, D.C.?

SOCIAL STUDIES
Quiz Whiz

Monticello was the home designed and built by what U.S. president?

SOCIAL STUDIES
Quiz Whiz

In which country would you find the Taj Mahal?

SOCIAL STUDIES
Quiz Whiz

What is the official song or anthem of the president of the United States?

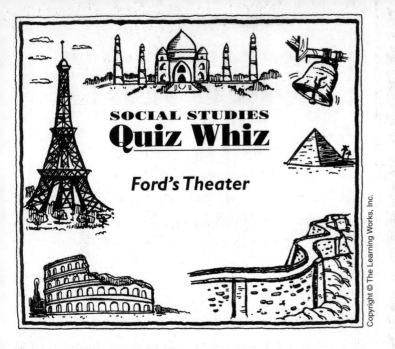

SOCIAL STUDIES Quiz Whiz

Ford's Theater

SOCIAL STUDIES Quiz Whiz

the 13 original colonies

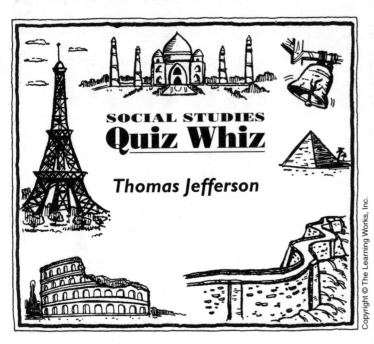

SOCIAL STUDIES Quiz Whiz

Thomas Jefferson

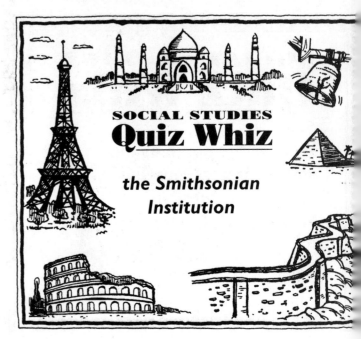

SOCIAL STUDIES Quiz Whiz

the Smithsonian Institution

SOCIAL STUDIES Quiz Whiz

"Hail to the Chief"

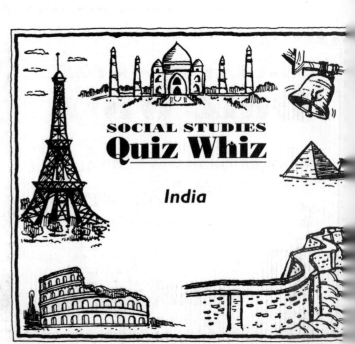

SOCIAL STUDIES Quiz Whiz

India

SOCIAL STUDIES
Quiz Whiz

In which country would you find the Suez Canal?

SOCIAL STUDIES
Quiz Whiz

In which city would you find the Golden Gate Bridge?

SOCIAL STUDIES
Quiz Whiz

In which country would you find the Wailing Wall?

SOCIAL STUDIES
Quiz Whiz

What statue was a gift from France and is the symbol of American freedom?

SOCIAL STUDIES
Quiz Whiz

In which Italian city would you find the Colosseum?

SOCIAL STUDIES
Quiz Whiz

In what state is Mount Rushmore located?

SOCIAL STUDIES
Quiz Whiz

*San Francisco,
California*

SOCIAL STUDIES
Quiz Whiz

Egypt

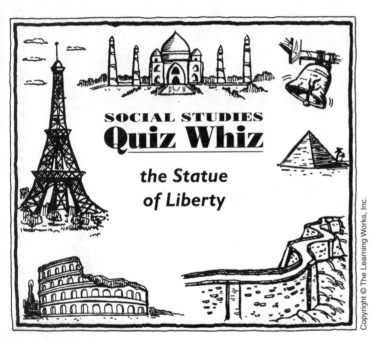

SOCIAL STUDIES
Quiz Whiz

*the Statue
of Liberty*

SOCIAL STUDIES
Quiz Whiz

Israel

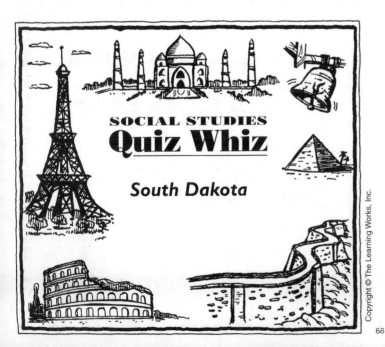

SOCIAL STUDIES
Quiz Whiz

South Dakota

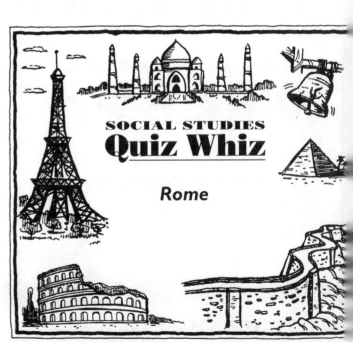

SOCIAL STUDIES
Quiz Whiz

Rome

SOCIAL STUDIES
Quiz Whiz

The sphinx in Egypt has the body of what animal?

SOCIAL STUDIES
Quiz Whiz

In what city and state is the Gateway Arch, the tallest monument in the United States?

SOCIAL STUDIES
Quiz Whiz

What famous gorge in Arizona was carved by the Colorado River?

SOCIAL STUDIES
Quiz Whiz

What do the letters D.C. stand for in the name Washington, D.C.?

SOCIAL STUDIES
Quiz Whiz

What is the name of the large clock on a tower near the Houses of Parliament in London?

SOCIAL STUDIES
Quiz Whiz

What is the name of the stone wall that stretches across northern China?

SOCIAL STUDIES
Quiz Whiz

St. Louis, Missouri

SOCIAL STUDIES
Quiz Whiz

lion

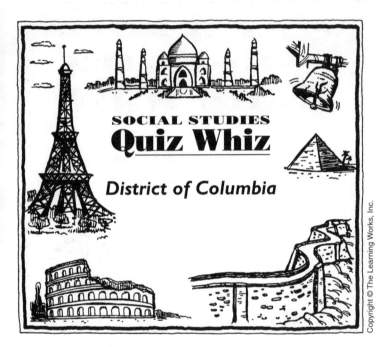

SOCIAL STUDIES
Quiz Whiz

District of Columbia

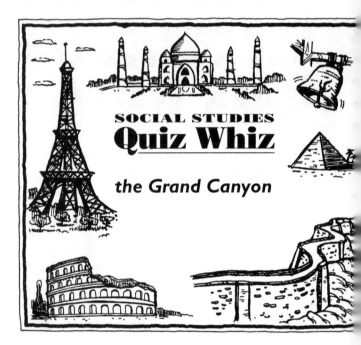

SOCIAL STUDIES
Quiz Whiz

the Grand Canyon

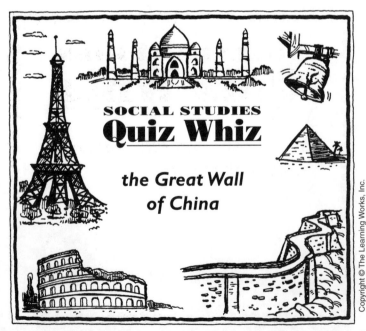

SOCIAL STUDIES
Quiz Whiz

the Great Wall of China

SOCIAL STUDIES
Quiz Whiz

Big Ben

SOCIAL STUDIES
Quiz Whiz

Is New Mexico north, south, east, or west of Arizona?

SOCIAL STUDIES
Quiz Whiz

Which state is directly north of Oregon?

SOCIAL STUDIES
Quiz Whiz

Is New Mexico north, south, east, or west of Colorado?

SOCIAL STUDIES
Quiz Whiz

Is Colorado north, south, east, or west of Kansas?

SOCIAL STUDIES
Quiz Whiz

Which state east of Vermont is nicknamed "The Granite State"?

SOCIAL STUDIES
Quiz Whiz

Is Ohio north, south, east, or west of Indiana?

SOCIAL STUDIES
Quiz Whiz

Washington

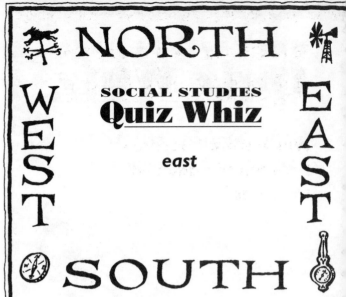

SOCIAL STUDIES
Quiz Whiz

east

SOCIAL STUDIES
Quiz Whiz

west

SOCIAL STUDIES
Quiz Whiz

south

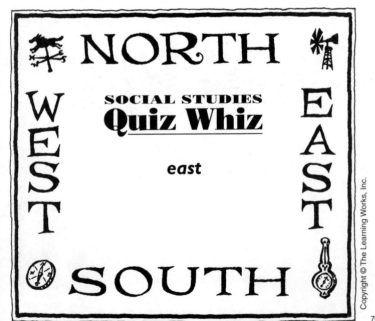

SOCIAL STUDIES
Quiz Whiz

east

SOCIAL STUDIES
Quiz Whiz

New Hampshire

SOCIAL STUDIES
Quiz Whiz

Which state is located between Nevada and Colorado?

SOCIAL STUDIES
Quiz Whiz

Is Illinois north, south, east, or west of Indiana?

SOCIAL STUDIES
Quiz Whiz

Which state located north of Pennsylvania is nicknamed "The Empire State"?

SOCIAL STUDIES
Quiz Whiz

Is Tennessee north, south, east, or west of Kentucky?

SOCIAL STUDIES
Quiz Whiz

Is Arkansas north, south, east, or west of Louisiana?

SOCIAL STUDIES
Quiz Whiz

Is Nevada north, south, east, or west of Utah?

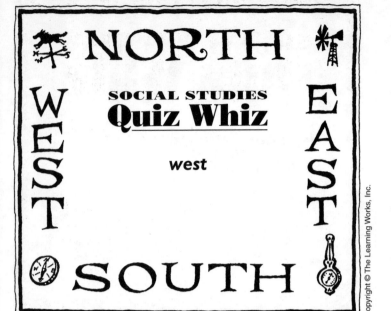

SOCIAL STUDIES
Quiz Whiz

west

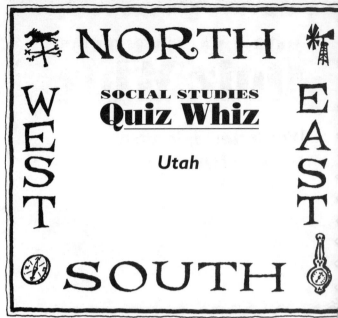

SOCIAL STUDIES
Quiz Whiz

Utah

SOCIAL STUDIES
Quiz Whiz

south

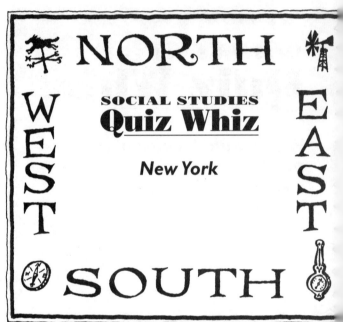

SOCIAL STUDIES
Quiz Whiz

New York

SOCIAL STUDIES
Quiz Whiz

west

SOCIAL STUDIES
Quiz Whiz

north

SOCIAL STUDIES
Quiz Whiz

Is Michigan north, south, east, or west of Indiana?

SOCIAL STUDIES
Quiz Whiz

Is Florida north, south, east, or west of Georgia?

SOCIAL STUDIES
Quiz Whiz

Which state contains the most easterly point in the United States?

SOCIAL STUDIES
Quiz Whiz

Is South Dakota north, south, east, or west of Nebraska?

SOCIAL STUDIES
Quiz Whiz

Is Utah north, south, east, or west of Idaho?

SOCIAL STUDIES
Quiz Whiz

Which state is directly north of California?

NORTH

WEST   EAST

SOCIAL STUDIES
Quiz Whiz

south

SOUTH

NORTH

WEST   EAST

SOCIAL STUDIES
Quiz Whiz

north

SOUTH

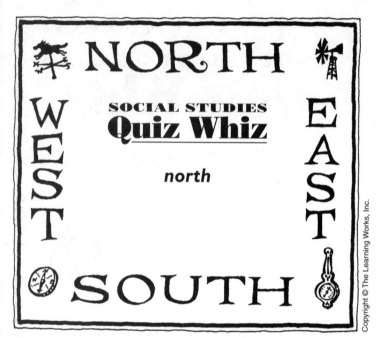

NORTH

WEST   EAST

SOCIAL STUDIES
Quiz Whiz

north

SOUTH

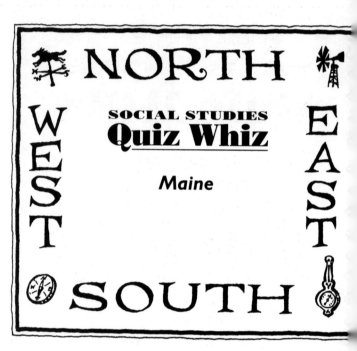

NORTH

WEST   EAST

SOCIAL STUDIES
Quiz Whiz

Maine

SOUTH

NORTH

WEST   EAST

SOCIAL STUDIES
Quiz Whiz

Oregon

SOUTH

NORTH

WEST   EAST

SOCIAL STUDIES
Quiz Whiz

south

SOUTH

SOCIAL STUDIES
Quiz Whiz

Which state east of New York is nicknamed "The Nutmeg State?"

SOCIAL STUDIES
Quiz Whiz

Is Maryland north, south, east, or west of Pennsylvania?

SOCIAL STUDIES
Quiz Whiz

Which state north of Texas is nicknamed "The Sooner State"?

SOCIAL STUDIES
Quiz Whiz

Is Kansas north, south, east, or west of Nebraska?

SOCIAL STUDIES
Quiz Whiz

Is Nebraska north, south, east, or west of Illinois?

SOCIAL STUDIES
Quiz Whiz

Is Oklahoma north, south, east, or west of Arkansas?

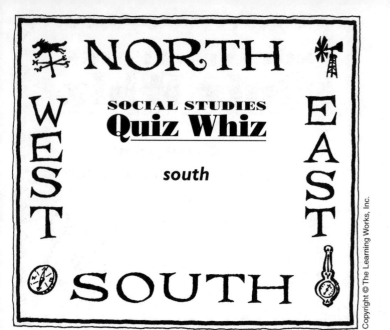

SOCIAL STUDIES
Quiz Whiz

NORTH

WEST

EAST

SOUTH

south

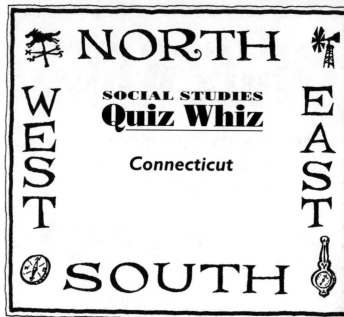

SOCIAL STUDIES
Quiz Whiz

NORTH

WEST

EAST

SOUTH

Connecticut

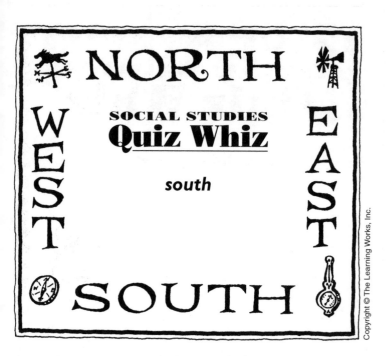

SOCIAL STUDIES
Quiz Whiz

NORTH

WEST

EAST

SOUTH

south

SOCIAL STUDIES
Quiz Whiz

NORTH

WEST

EAST

SOUTH

Oklahoma

SOCIAL STUDIES
Quiz Whiz

NORTH

WEST

EAST

SOUTH

west

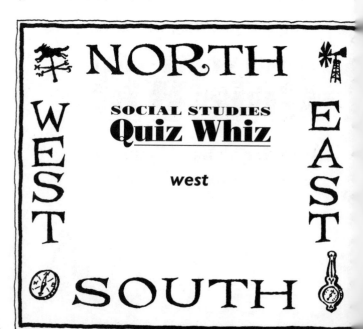

SOCIAL STUDIES
Quiz Whiz

NORTH

WEST

EAST

SOUTH

west

SOCIAL STUDIES
Quiz Whiz

Which state is farthest west: Illinois, Louisiana, Alabama, or New Mexico?

SOCIAL STUDIES
Quiz Whiz

Which state is between Georgia and North Carolina?

SOCIAL STUDIES
Quiz Whiz

Is Arkansas north, south, east, or west of Missouri?

SOCIAL STUDIES
Quiz Whiz

Which state is between Massachusetts and Connecticut?

SOCIAL STUDIES
Quiz Whiz

Is Wisconsin north, south, east, or west of South Dakota?

SOCIAL STUDIES
Quiz Whiz

Which state is farthest east: Texas, South Carolina, Mississippi, or Tennessee?

SOCIAL STUDIES
Quiz Whiz

South Carolina

SOCIAL STUDIES
Quiz Whiz

New Mexico

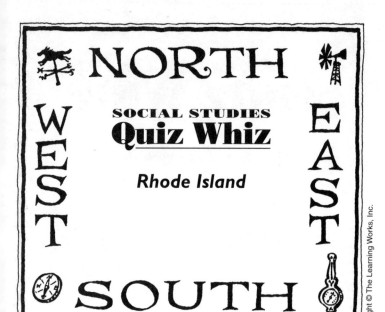

SOCIAL STUDIES
Quiz Whiz

Rhode Island

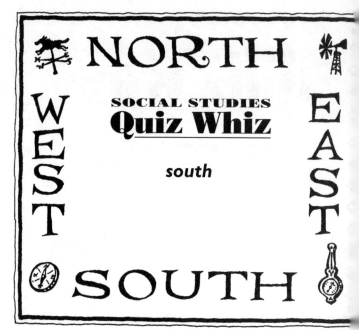

SOCIAL STUDIES
Quiz Whiz

south

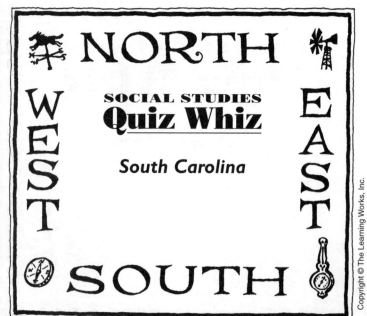

SOCIAL STUDIES
Quiz Whiz

South Carolina

SOCIAL STUDIES
Quiz Whiz

east

SOCIAL STUDIES
Quiz Whiz

Is Alabama north, south, east, or west of Louisiana?

SOCIAL STUDIES
Quiz Whiz

Which state is farthest west: Kentucky, Tennessee, Kansas, or Alabama?

SOCIAL STUDIES
Quiz Whiz

Is California north, south, east, or west of Washington?

SOCIAL STUDIES
Quiz Whiz

Which state is farthest north: Ohio, Indiana, Illinois, or Michigan?

SOCIAL STUDIES
Quiz Whiz

Is Idaho north, south, east, or west of Oregon?

SOCIAL STUDIES
Quiz Whiz

Which state is farthest south: Arizona, Utah, Colorado, or Nevada?

SOCIAL STUDIES
Quiz Whiz

Kansas

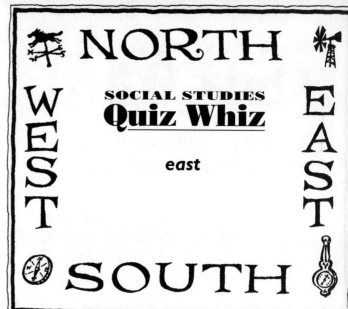

SOCIAL STUDIES
Quiz Whiz

east

SOCIAL STUDIES
Quiz Whiz

Michigan

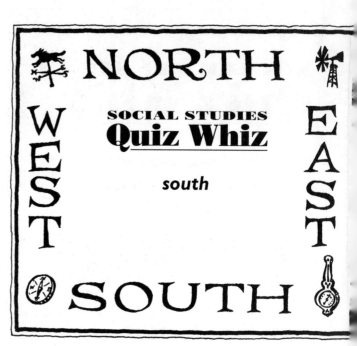

SOCIAL STUDIES
Quiz Whiz

south

SOCIAL STUDIES
Quiz Whiz

Arizona

SOCIAL STUDIES
Quiz Whiz

east

SOCIAL STUDIES
Quiz Whiz

Who was the first president of the United States?

SOCIAL STUDIES
Quiz Whiz

Who became president of the United States after Bill Clinton?

SOCIAL STUDIES
Quiz Whiz

Who was the youngest man ever to be elected president of the United States?

SOCIAL STUDIES
Quiz Whiz

Who became president after the assassination of John Kennedy?

SOCIAL STUDIES
Quiz Whiz

Who was president of the United States during World War I?

SOCIAL STUDIES
Quiz Whiz

Which president had a wife whose name was Mamie?

SOCIAL STUDIES
Quiz Whiz
George W. Bush

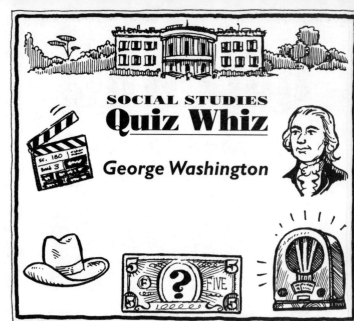

SOCIAL STUDIES
Quiz Whiz
George Washington

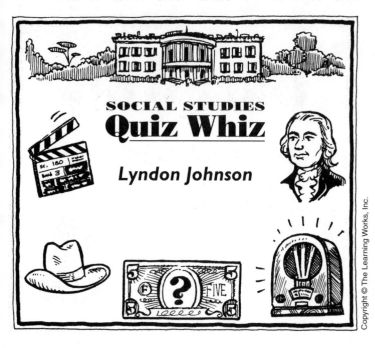

SOCIAL STUDIES
Quiz Whiz
Lyndon Johnson

SOCIAL STUDIES
Quiz Whiz
John Kennedy

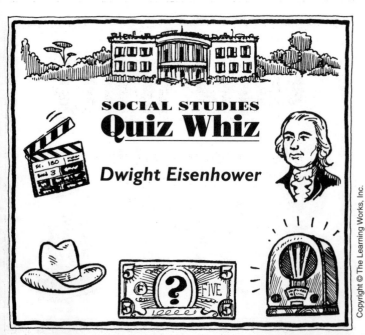

SOCIAL STUDIES
Quiz Whiz
Dwight Eisenhower

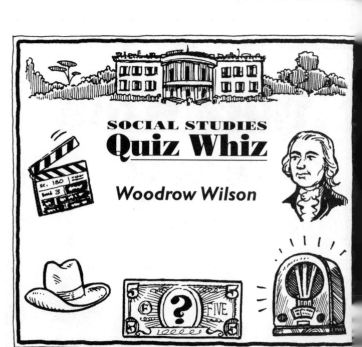

SOCIAL STUDIES
Quiz Whiz
Woodrow Wilson

SOCIAL STUDIES
Quiz Whiz

Who was president between Jimmy Carter and George H.W. Bush?

SOCIAL STUDIES
Quiz Whiz

Which U.S. president is pictured on the dime?

SOCIAL STUDIES
Quiz Whiz

The president of the United States is elected to serve for how many years?

SOCIAL STUDIES
Quiz Whiz

Which U.S. president is pictured on the one-dollar bill?

SOCIAL STUDIES
Quiz Whiz

Who was president when the White House was burned by the British in 1814?

SOCIAL STUDIES
Quiz Whiz

Before becoming president, George H.W. Bush served as vice president under which president?

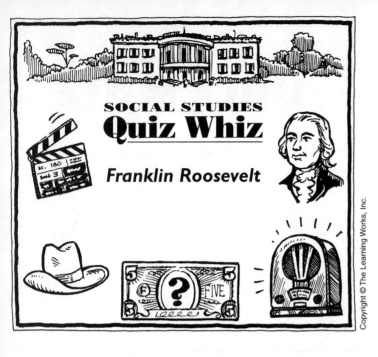

SOCIAL STUDIES
Quiz Whiz

Franklin Roosevelt

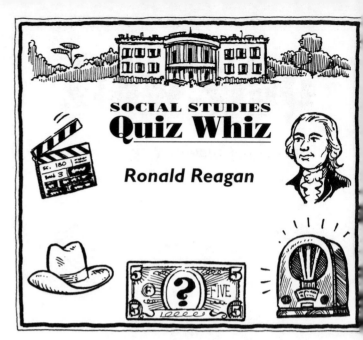

SOCIAL STUDIES
Quiz Whiz

Ronald Reagan

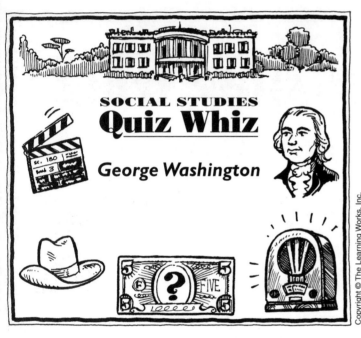

SOCIAL STUDIES
Quiz Whiz

George Washington

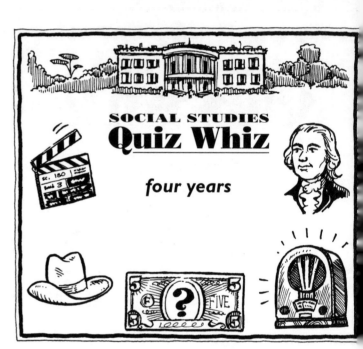

SOCIAL STUDIES
Quiz Whiz

four years

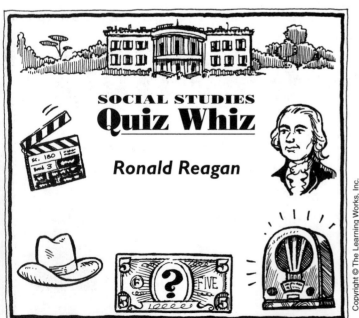

SOCIAL STUDIES
Quiz Whiz

Ronald Reagan

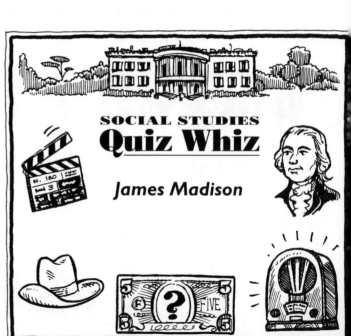

SOCIAL STUDIES
Quiz Whiz

James Madison

SOCIAL STUDIES
Quiz Whiz

Which president began a speech with the words "Fourscore and seven years ago…"?

SOCIAL STUDIES
Quiz Whiz

Which president was assassinated by Lee Harvey Oswald on November 22, 1963?

SOCIAL STUDIES
Quiz Whiz

Which U.S. president's picture is on the nickel?

SOCIAL STUDIES
Quiz Whiz

Which president had a wife whose name was Claudia but was called Lady Bird?

SOCIAL STUDIES
Quiz Whiz

Who was the first president to live in the White House?

SOCIAL STUDIES
Quiz Whiz

Richard Nixon served as vice president to which president?

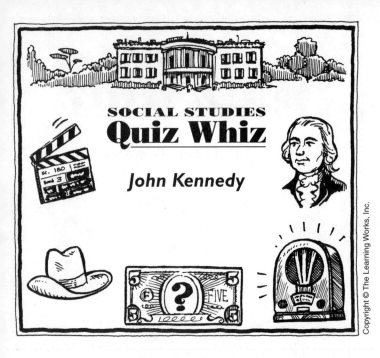

SOCIAL STUDIES
Quiz Whiz
John Kennedy

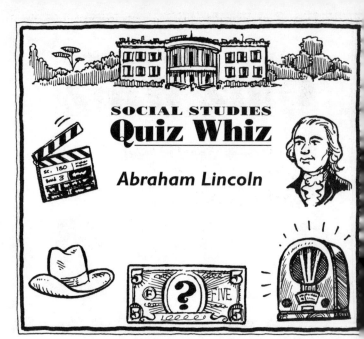

SOCIAL STUDIES
Quiz Whiz
Abraham Lincoln

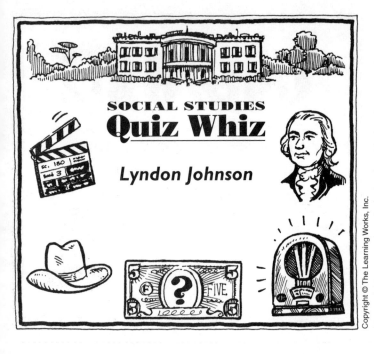

SOCIAL STUDIES
Quiz Whiz
Lyndon Johnson

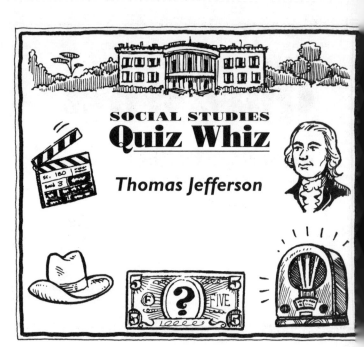

SOCIAL STUDIES
Quiz Whiz
Thomas Jefferson

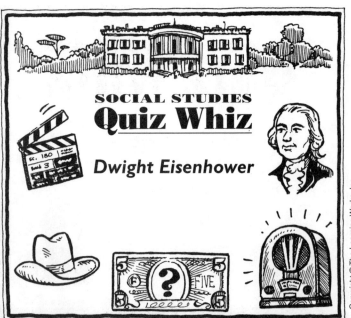

SOCIAL STUDIES
Quiz Whiz
Dwight Eisenhower

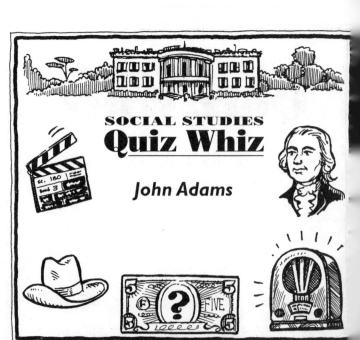

SOCIAL STUDIES
Quiz Whiz
John Adams

SOCIAL STUDIES
Quiz Whiz

Which U.S. president
is pictured on the
five-dollar bill?

SOCIAL STUDIES
Quiz Whiz

Which president established
the New Deal following
the Great Depression?

SOCIAL STUDIES
Quiz Whiz

Which president had a wife
who later became a
U.S. Senator?

SOCIAL STUDIES
Quiz Whiz

Which of the following never
served as president: Benjamin
Franklin, James Monroe,
John Tyler, or
William Taft?

SOCIAL STUDIES
Quiz Whiz

Who was the only president
elected to four terms
in office?

SOCIAL STUDIES
Quiz Whiz

Which president was
commander of the
Union Army in the
Civil War?

SOCIAL STUDIES
Quiz Whiz

Franklin Roosevelt

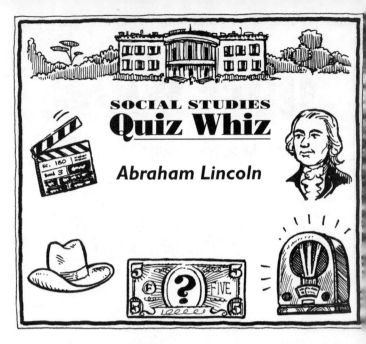

SOCIAL STUDIES
Quiz Whiz

Abraham Lincoln

SOCIAL STUDIES
Quiz Whiz

Benjamin Franklin

SOCIAL STUDIES
Quiz Whiz

Bill Clinton

SOCIAL STUDIES
Quiz Whiz

Ulysses Grant

SOCIAL STUDIES
Quiz Whiz

Franklin Roosevelt

SOCIAL STUDIES
Quiz Whiz

Which president was a peanut farmer before taking office?

SOCIAL STUDIES
Quiz Whiz

Who was the first president to resign his office?

SOCIAL STUDIES
Quiz Whiz

Which president served the shortest time in office?

SOCIAL STUDIES
Quiz Whiz

Who was the first president to speak on the radio: William Taft, Woodrow Wilson, Warren Harding, or Calvin Coolidge?

SOCIAL STUDIES
Quiz Whiz

Who was the only president who was the grandson of a president?

SOCIAL STUDIES
Quiz Whiz

Who served as vice president under Bill Clinton?

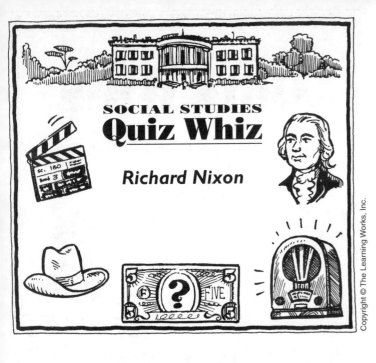

SOCIAL STUDIES
Quiz Whiz

Richard Nixon

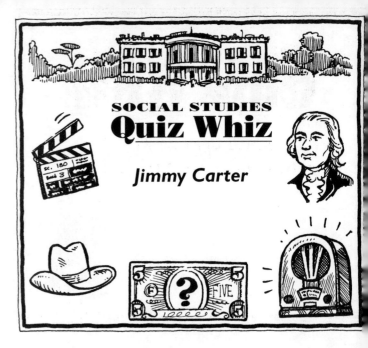

SOCIAL STUDIES
Quiz Whiz

Jimmy Carter

SOCIAL STUDIES
Quiz Whiz

Woodrow Wilson

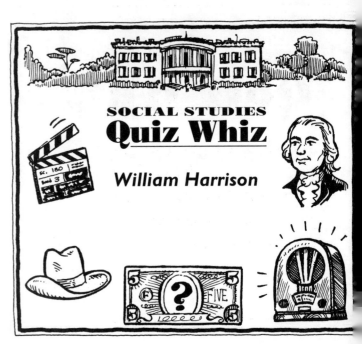

SOCIAL STUDIES
Quiz Whiz

William Harrison

SOCIAL STUDIES
Quiz Whiz

Al Gore

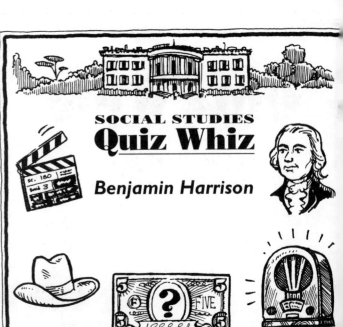

SOCIAL STUDIES
Quiz Whiz

Benjamin Harrison

SOCIAL STUDIES
Quiz Whiz

Which president had a wife whose name was Eleanor?

SOCIAL STUDIES
Quiz Whiz

Which president worked as an actor in Hollywood before becoming president?

SOCIAL STUDIES
Quiz Whiz

Which of the following was the only president who never married: Andrew Johnson, James Buchanan, or James Garfield?

SOCIAL STUDIES
Quiz Whiz

Who was the first Roman Catholic president?

SOCIAL STUDIES
Quiz Whiz

Which president had the most children?

SOCIAL STUDIES
Quiz Whiz

Dan Quayle served as vice president under which president?

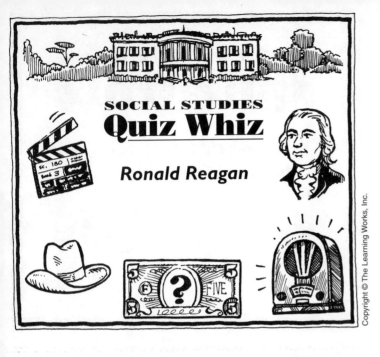

SOCIAL STUDIES
Quiz Whiz
Ronald Reagan

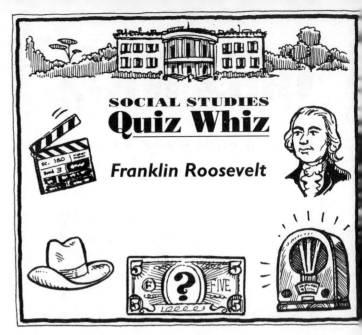

SOCIAL STUDIES
Quiz Whiz
Franklin Roosevelt

SOCIAL STUDIES
Quiz Whiz
John Kennedy

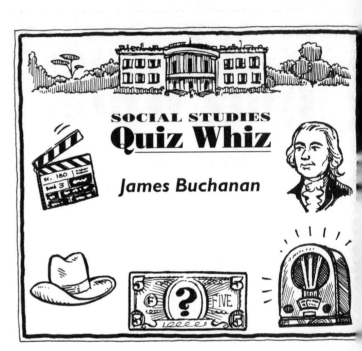

SOCIAL STUDIES
Quiz Whiz
James Buchanan

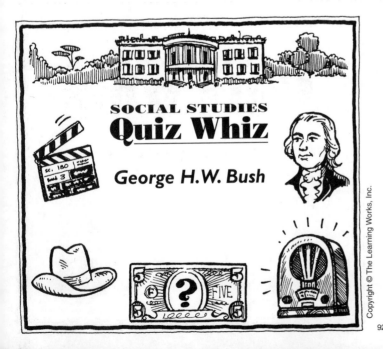

SOCIAL STUDIES
Quiz Whiz
George H.W. Bush

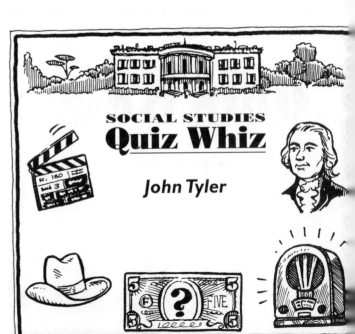

SOCIAL STUDIES
Quiz Whiz
John Tyler

SOCIAL STUDIES
Quiz Whiz

Dover is the capital of which state?

SOCIAL STUDIES
Quiz Whiz

Springfield is the capital of which state?

SOCIAL STUDIES
Quiz Whiz

What is the capital of Oklahoma?

SOCIAL STUDIES
Quiz Whiz

Hartford is the capital of which state?

SOCIAL STUDIES
Quiz Whiz

What is the capital of Indiana?

SOCIAL STUDIES
Quiz Whiz

Salem is the capital of which state?

SOCIAL STUDIES
Quiz Whiz

Illinois

SOCIAL STUDIES
Quiz Whiz

Delaware

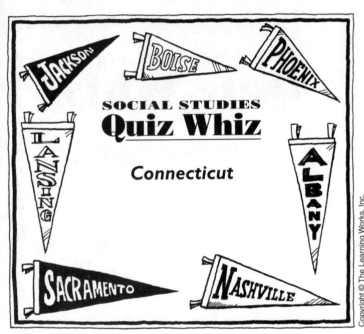

SOCIAL STUDIES
Quiz Whiz

Connecticut

SOCIAL STUDIES
Quiz Whiz

Oklahoma City

SOCIAL STUDIES
Quiz Whiz

Oregon

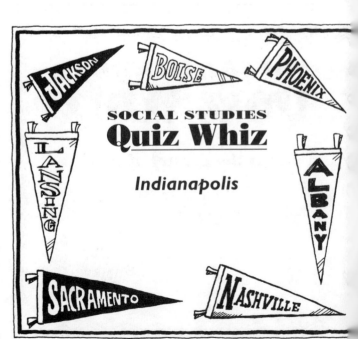

SOCIAL STUDIES
Quiz Whiz

Indianapolis

SOCIAL STUDIES Quiz Whiz

Pierre is the capital of which state?

SOCIAL STUDIES Quiz Whiz

Cheyenne is the capital of which state, nicknamed "The Equality State"?

SOCIAL STUDIES Quiz Whiz

Montpelier is the capital of which state, nicknamed "The Green Mountain State"?

SOCIAL STUDIES Quiz Whiz

Baton Rouge is the capital of which state, nicknamed "The Pelican State"?

SOCIAL STUDIES Quiz Whiz

Jefferson City is the capital of which state, the boyhood home of Mark Twain?

SOCIAL STUDIES Quiz Whiz

Boise is the capital of which state, whose state bird is the mountain bluebird?

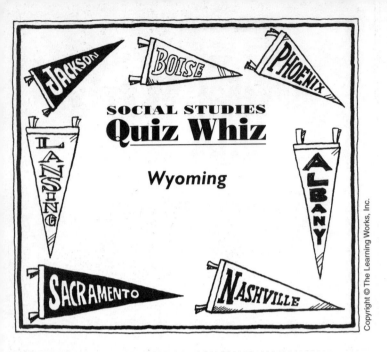

SOCIAL STUDIES
Quiz Whiz
Wyoming

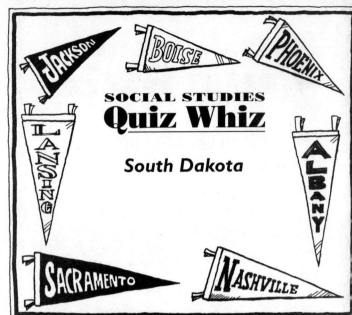

SOCIAL STUDIES
Quiz Whiz
South Dakota

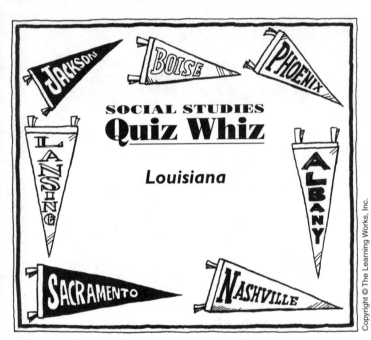

SOCIAL STUDIES
Quiz Whiz
Louisiana

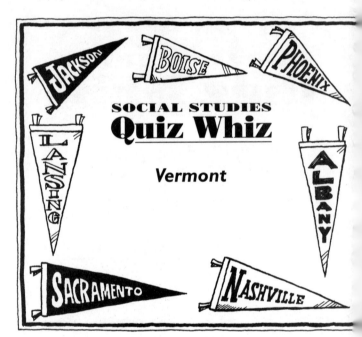

SOCIAL STUDIES
Quiz Whiz
Vermont

SOCIAL STUDIES
Quiz Whiz
Idaho

SOCIAL STUDIES
Quiz Whiz
Missouri

SOCIAL STUDIES
Quiz Whiz

Madison is the capital of which state, known as "The Badger State"?

SOCIAL STUDIES
Quiz Whiz

Phoenix is the capital of which state, nicknamed "The Grand Canyon State"?

SOCIAL STUDIES
Quiz Whiz

Lincoln is the capital of which state, whose largest city is Omaha?

SOCIAL STUDIES
Quiz Whiz

What is the capital of Alabama?

SOCIAL STUDIES
Quiz Whiz

Frankfort is the capital of which state?

SOCIAL STUDIES
Quiz Whiz

Sacramento is the capital of which state?

SOCIAL STUDIES
Quiz Whiz

Arizona

SOCIAL STUDIES
Quiz Whiz

Wisconsin

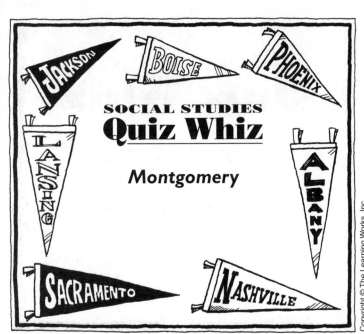

SOCIAL STUDIES
Quiz Whiz

Montgomery

SOCIAL STUDIES
Quiz Whiz

Nebraska

SOCIAL STUDIES
Quiz Whiz

California

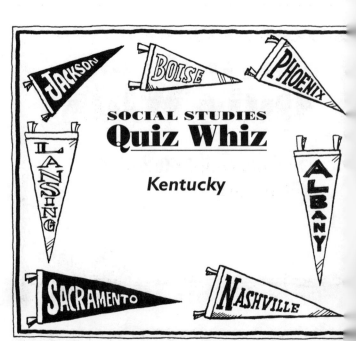

SOCIAL STUDIES
Quiz Whiz

Kentucky

SOCIAL STUDIES
Quiz Whiz

Des Moines is the capital of which state, nicknamed "The Hawkeye State"?

SOCIAL STUDIES
Quiz Whiz

Trenton is the capital of which state, whose largest city is Newark?

SOCIAL STUDIES
Quiz Whiz

What is the capital of Arkansas?

SOCIAL STUDIES
Quiz Whiz

Santa Fe is the capital of which state, that has the roadrunner as its state bird?

SOCIAL STUDIES
Quiz Whiz

Olympia is the capital of which state?

SOCIAL STUDIES
Quiz Whiz

Annapolis is the capital of which state?

SOCIAL STUDIES
Quiz Whiz

New Jersey

SOCIAL STUDIES
Quiz Whiz

Iowa

SOCIAL STUDIES
Quiz Whiz

New Mexico

SOCIAL STUDIES
Quiz Whiz

Little Rock

SOCIAL STUDIES
Quiz Whiz

Maryland

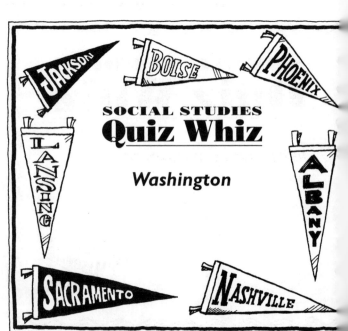

SOCIAL STUDIES
Quiz Whiz

Washington

SOCIAL STUDIES
Quiz Whiz

What is the capital of North Carolina?

SOCIAL STUDIES
Quiz Whiz

Nashville is the capital of which state, nicknamed "The Volunteer State"?

SOCIAL STUDIES
Quiz Whiz

What is the capital of Maine?

SOCIAL STUDIES
Quiz Whiz

Austin is the capital of which state?

SOCIAL STUDIES
Quiz Whiz

What is the capital of Ohio?

SOCIAL STUDIES
Quiz Whiz

Albany is the capital of which state?

SOCIAL STUDIES
Quiz Whiz

Tennessee

SOCIAL STUDIES
Quiz Whiz

Raleigh

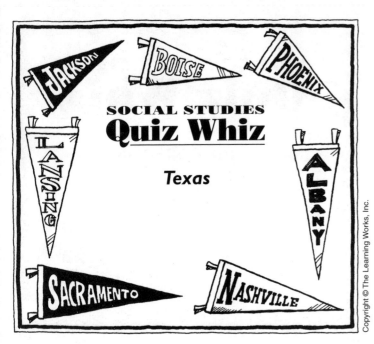

SOCIAL STUDIES
Quiz Whiz

Texas

SOCIAL STUDIES
Quiz Whiz

Augusta

SOCIAL STUDIES
Quiz Whiz

New York

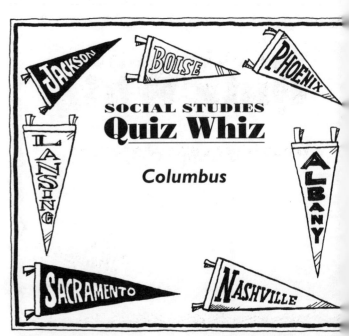

SOCIAL STUDIES
Quiz Whiz

Columbus

SOCIAL STUDIES
Quiz Whiz

What is the capital of Alaska?

SOCIAL STUDIES
Quiz Whiz

Harrisburg is the capital of which state?

SOCIAL STUDIES
Quiz Whiz

What is the capital of Virginia?

SOCIAL STUDIES
Quiz Whiz

Helena is the capital of which state?

SOCIAL STUDIES
Quiz Whiz

What is the capital of Utah?

SOCIAL STUDIES
Quiz Whiz

Lansing is the capital of which state?

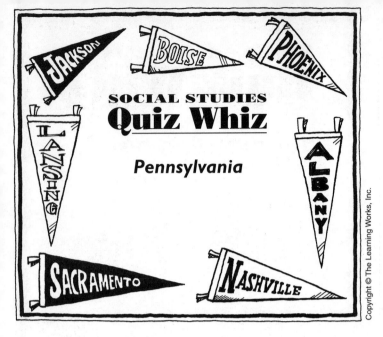

SOCIAL STUDIES
Quiz Whiz

Pennsylvania

SOCIAL STUDIES
Quiz Whiz

Juneau

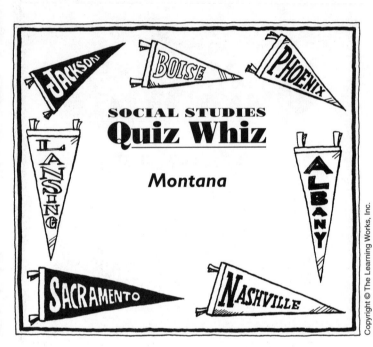

SOCIAL STUDIES
Quiz Whiz

Montana

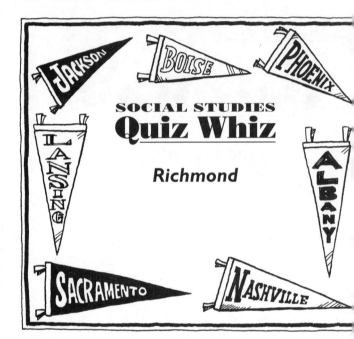

SOCIAL STUDIES
Quiz Whiz

Richmond

SOCIAL STUDIES
Quiz Whiz

Michigan

SOCIAL STUDIES
Quiz Whiz

Salt Lake City

SOCIAL STUDIES
Quiz Whiz

Which is not a New England state: Maryland, Rhode Island, or Massachusetts?

SOCIAL STUDIES
Quiz Whiz

What term describes a stream or small river that flows into a larger river?

SOCIAL STUDIES
Quiz Whiz

Which is the highest mountain in the United States?

SOCIAL STUDIES
Quiz Whiz

What four states meet at Four Corners?

SOCIAL STUDIES
Quiz Whiz

In which state is the Mojave Desert found?

SOCIAL STUDIES
Quiz Whiz

Which is the largest of the five Great Lakes?

SOCIAL STUDIES
Quiz Whiz

a tributary

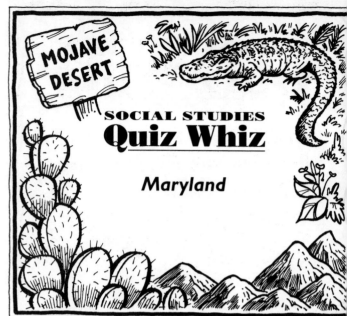

SOCIAL STUDIES
Quiz Whiz

Maryland

SOCIAL STUDIES
Quiz Whiz

*Arizona, Utah,
Colorado, and
New Mexico*

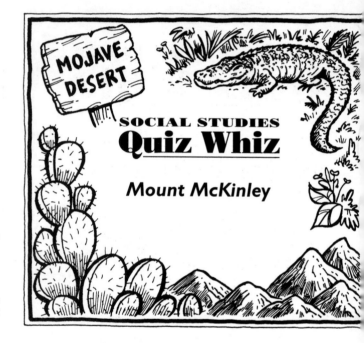

SOCIAL STUDIES
Quiz Whiz

Mount McKinley

SOCIAL STUDIES
Quiz Whiz

Lake Superior

SOCIAL STUDIES
Quiz Whiz

California

SOCIAL STUDIES
Quiz Whiz

What U.S. city is known as the "Mile High City"?

SOCIAL STUDIES
Quiz Whiz

What is the term used for a piece of land that is surrounded on three sides by water?

SOCIAL STUDIES
Quiz Whiz

Which is not a middle Atlantic state: New York, New Jersey, or Kentucky?

SOCIAL STUDIES
Quiz Whiz

What term applies to a narrow channel of water that connects two large bodies of water?

SOCIAL STUDIES
Quiz Whiz

What ocean borders the U.S. on the east coast?

SOCIAL STUDIES
Quiz Whiz

In which state is Yosemite National Park located?

SOCIAL STUDIES
Quiz Whiz

a peninsula

SOCIAL STUDIES
Quiz Whiz

Denver, Colorado

SOCIAL STUDIES
Quiz Whiz

a strait

SOCIAL STUDIES
Quiz Whiz

Kentucky

SOCIAL STUDIES
Quiz Whiz

California

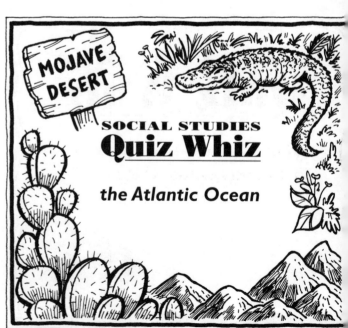

SOCIAL STUDIES
Quiz Whiz

the Atlantic Ocean

SOCIAL STUDIES
Quiz Whiz

What is the longest river in the United States?

SOCIAL STUDIES
Quiz Whiz

In the continental U.S., which state has the fewest states on its border?

SOCIAL STUDIES
Quiz Whiz

What term is applied to a narrow strip of land that connects two large bodies of land?

SOCIAL STUDIES
Quiz Whiz

Which is not a southwestern state: Idaho, Oklahoma, or New Mexico?

SOCIAL STUDIES
Quiz Whiz

What term describes a place in a desert where there is a natural spring?

SOCIAL STUDIES
Quiz Whiz

What is the name of the body of seawater along the southern U.S. and Mexico?

SOCIAL STUDIES
Quiz Whiz

Maine

SOCIAL STUDIES
Quiz Whiz

the Mississippi River

SOCIAL STUDIES
Quiz Whiz

Idaho

SOCIAL STUDIES
Quiz Whiz

an isthmus

SOCIAL STUDIES
Quiz Whiz

the Gulf of Mexico

SOCIAL STUDIES
Quiz Whiz

an oasis

SOCIAL STUDIES
Quiz Whiz

What is a sheltered body of water called where ships can safely anchor?

SOCIAL STUDIES
Quiz Whiz

What do you call a large ice mass that moves slowly down a mountain or over land?

SOCIAL STUDIES
Quiz Whiz

What is the term for a man-made waterway that is used for shipping, travel, or irrigation?

SOCIAL STUDIES
Quiz Whiz

What body of water, off the west coast of the U.S., is the world's largest and deepest?

SOCIAL STUDIES
Quiz Whiz

What is the low land called between mountains or hills?

SOCIAL STUDIES
Quiz Whiz

Which is not a western state: California, New Mexico, or Nevada?

SOCIAL STUDIES
Quiz Whiz

a glacier

SOCIAL STUDIES
Quiz Whiz

a harbor

SOCIAL STUDIES
Quiz Whiz

the Pacific Ocean

SOCIAL STUDIES
Quiz Whiz

a canal

SOCIAL STUDIES
Quiz Whiz

New Mexico

SOCIAL STUDIES
Quiz Whiz

a valley

SOCIAL STUDIES
Quiz Whiz

What is the term for a triangular area of land that is formed by deposits at the mouth of a river?

SOCIAL STUDIES
Quiz Whiz

Where in North America is Mt. McKinley located?

SOCIAL STUDIES
Quiz Whiz

Is "Sierra Nevada" the name of a river, a lake, a mountain range, or a city?

SOCIAL STUDIES
Quiz Whiz

In which state is Everglades National Park located?

SOCIAL STUDIES
Quiz Whiz

Which is not a southern state: Georgia, Nebraska, Florida, or Alabama?

SOCIAL STUDIES
Quiz Whiz

What term is applied to a large area of flat land that is higher than the surrounding region?

SOCIAL STUDIES
Quiz Whiz

Alaska

SOCIAL STUDIES
Quiz Whiz

a delta

SOCIAL STUDIES
Quiz Whiz

Florida

SOCIAL STUDIES
Quiz Whiz

a mountain range

SOCIAL STUDIES
Quiz Whiz

a plateau

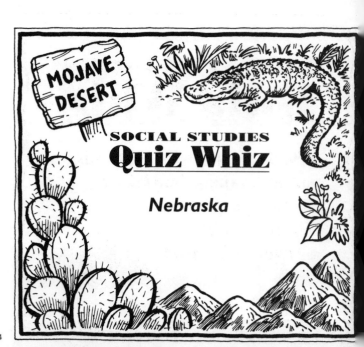

SOCIAL STUDIES
Quiz Whiz

Nebraska

SOCIAL STUDIES
Quiz Whiz

What is the term for a dry area of land where few plants grow?

SOCIAL STUDIES
Quiz Whiz

Which state is home to the Arctic National Wildlife Refuge?

SOCIAL STUDIES
Quiz Whiz

Which is not one of the Great Lakes: Erie, Ohio, Michigan, or Huron?

SOCIAL STUDIES
Quiz Whiz

Which country borders the United States on the north?

SOCIAL STUDIES
Quiz Whiz

Which of these mountains is not located in the United States: Pike's Peak, Mount Everest, or Mount Shasta?

SOCIAL STUDIES
Quiz Whiz

Which of the following rivers is not found in the United States: Niger, Missouri, or Yukon?

SOCIAL STUDIES
Quiz Whiz

Alaska

SOCIAL STUDIES
Quiz Whiz

a desert

SOCIAL STUDIES
Quiz Whiz

Canada

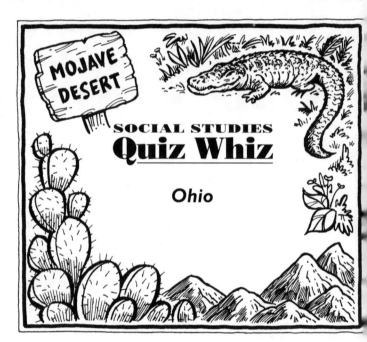

SOCIAL STUDIES
Quiz Whiz

Ohio

SOCIAL STUDIES
Quiz Whiz

Niger

SOCIAL STUDIES
Quiz Whiz

Mount Everest

SOCIAL STUDIES
Quiz Whiz

On which continent would you find the Sahara Desert?

SOCIAL STUDIES
Quiz Whiz

Which continent has the smallest area?

SOCIAL STUDIES
Quiz Whiz

Which lake, on the border between Israel and Jordan, is the saltiest lake in the world?

SOCIAL STUDIES
Quiz Whiz

Which continent has the largest area?

SOCIAL STUDIES
Quiz Whiz

Which country is not part of South America: India, Venezuela, Argentina, or Ecuador?

SOCIAL STUDIES
Quiz Whiz

What is another name for The Netherlands?

SOCIAL STUDIES
Quiz Whiz

Australia

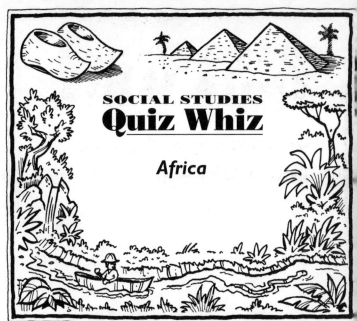

SOCIAL STUDIES
Quiz Whiz

Africa

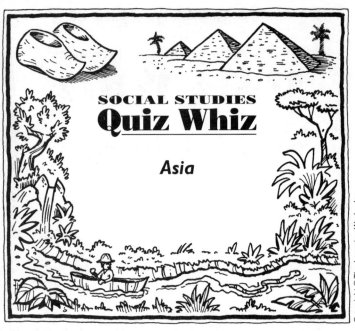

SOCIAL STUDIES
Quiz Whiz

Asia

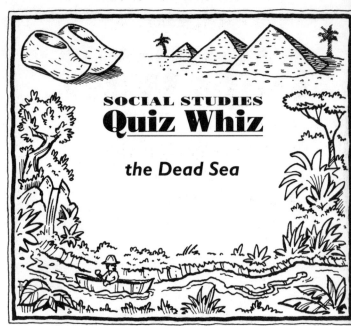

SOCIAL STUDIES
Quiz Whiz

the Dead Sea

SOCIAL STUDIES
Quiz Whiz

Holland

SOCIAL STUDIES
Quiz Whiz

India

SOCIAL STUDIES
Quiz Whiz

What is the highest mountain in the world?

SOCIAL STUDIES
Quiz Whiz

Which is the smallest ocean in the world?

SOCIAL STUDIES
Quiz Whiz

The Himalaya mountain range is located on which continent?

SOCIAL STUDIES
Quiz Whiz

On which continent is Egypt?

SOCIAL STUDIES
Quiz Whiz

If you were in the city of Budapest, in which country would you be?

SOCIAL STUDIES
Quiz Whiz

Which country is not located in North America: Canada, the United States, Mexico, or Paraguay?

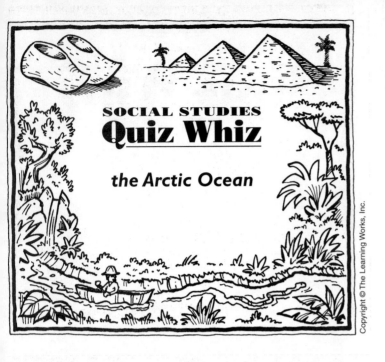

SOCIAL STUDIES
Quiz Whiz

the Arctic Ocean

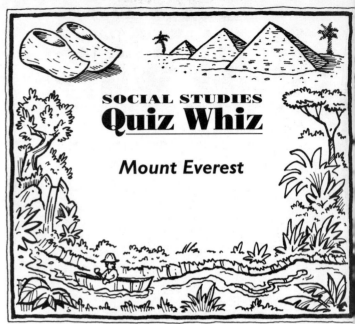

SOCIAL STUDIES
Quiz Whiz

Mount Everest

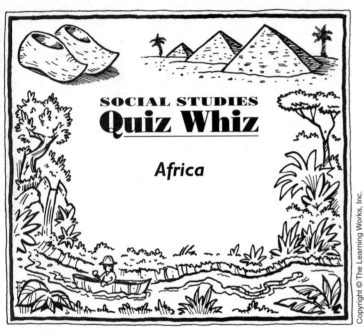

SOCIAL STUDIES
Quiz Whiz

Africa

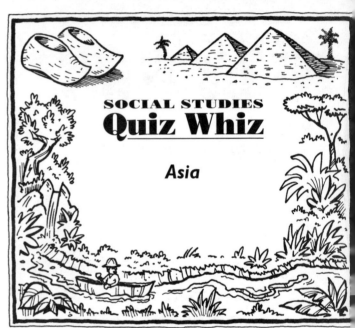

SOCIAL STUDIES
Quiz Whiz

Asia

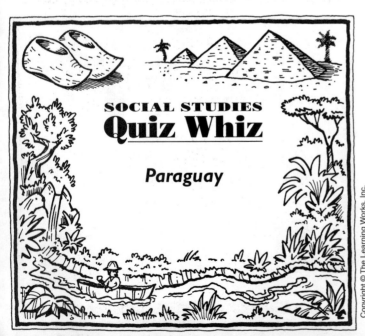

SOCIAL STUDIES
Quiz Whiz

Paraguay

SOCIAL STUDIES
Quiz Whiz

Hungary

SOCIAL STUDIES
Quiz Whiz

What is the longest river in the world?

SOCIAL STUDIES
Quiz Whiz

In which country would you find the cities of Tel Aviv, Jerusalem, and Haifa?

SOCIAL STUDIES
Quiz Whiz

What is the largest island in the world?

SOCIAL STUDIES
Quiz Whiz

Which country is not part of Africa: Mongolia, Sudan, Ethiopia, or Libya?

SOCIAL STUDIES
Quiz Whiz

In what country is Hanoi?

SOCIAL STUDIES
Quiz Whiz

The Yangtze River is the longest river and most important waterway of which Asian country?

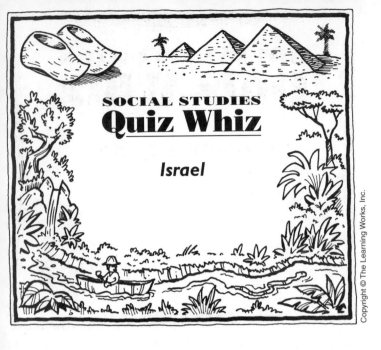

SOCIAL STUDIES
Quiz Whiz

Israel

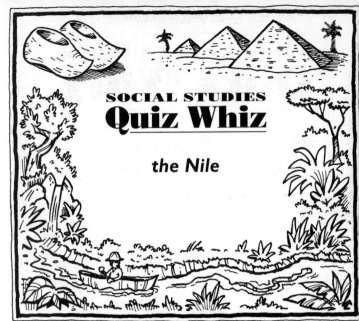

SOCIAL STUDIES
Quiz Whiz

the Nile

SOCIAL STUDIES
Quiz Whiz

Mongolia

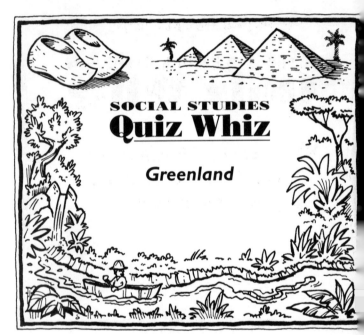

SOCIAL STUDIES
Quiz Whiz

Greenland

SOCIAL STUDIES
Quiz Whiz

China

SOCIAL STUDIES
Quiz Whiz

Vietnam

SOCIAL STUDIES
Quiz Whiz

What cape at the tip of Chile is known for its fierce storms and violent seas?

SOCIAL STUDIES
Quiz Whiz

What is the largest gulf in the world?

SOCIAL STUDIES
Quiz Whiz

Which country is called the "Emerald Isle" because of its lush green countryside?

SOCIAL STUDIES
Quiz Whiz

What sea separates Alaska and Russia?

SOCIAL STUDIES
Quiz Whiz

Which country is not part of Europe: France, Turkey, Spain, Switzerland, or Italy?

SOCIAL STUDIES
Quiz Whiz

Mount Kilimanjaro is located on which continent?

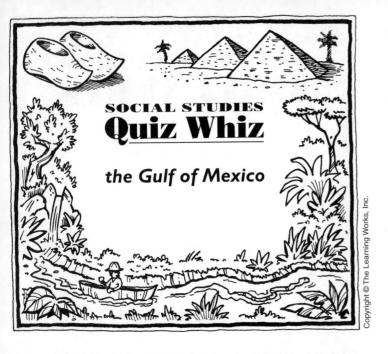

SOCIAL STUDIES
Quiz Whiz

the Gulf of Mexico

SOCIAL STUDIES
Quiz Whiz

Cape Horn

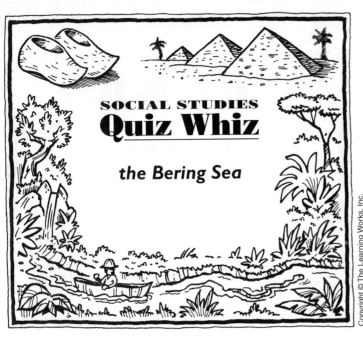

SOCIAL STUDIES
Quiz Whiz

the Bering Sea

SOCIAL STUDIES
Quiz Whiz

Ireland

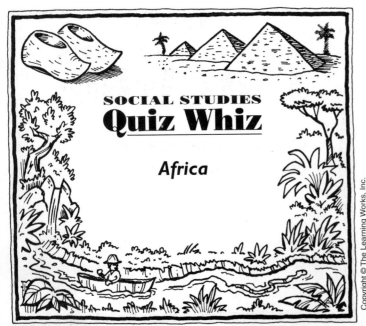

SOCIAL STUDIES
Quiz Whiz

Africa

SOCIAL STUDIES
Quiz Whiz

Turkey

SOCIAL STUDIES
Quiz Whiz

If you were in the city of Tijuana, in which country would you be?

SOCIAL STUDIES
Quiz Whiz

What is the largest city and capital of Greece?

SOCIAL STUDIES
Quiz Whiz

What is the name of Europe's longest river?

SOCIAL STUDIES
Quiz Whiz

Which country is not part of Africa: Niger, Egypt, Angola, or Iraq?

SOCIAL STUDIES
Quiz Whiz

Which is not part of Great Britain: Wales, Scotland, Norway, or England?

SOCIAL STUDIES
Quiz Whiz

On which continent is the Cape of Good Hope?

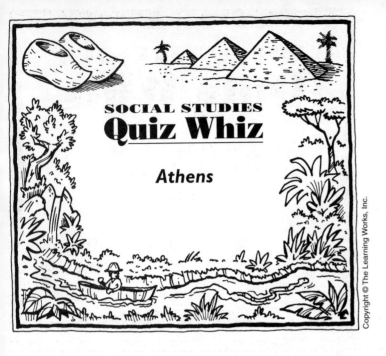

SOCIAL STUDIES
Quiz Whiz

Athens

SOCIAL STUDIES
Quiz Whiz

Mexico

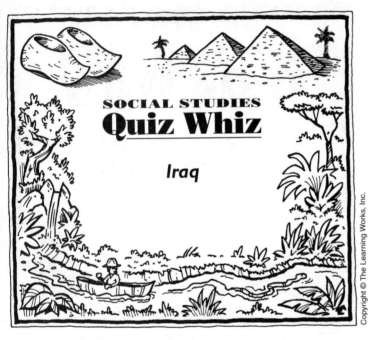

SOCIAL STUDIES
Quiz Whiz

Iraq

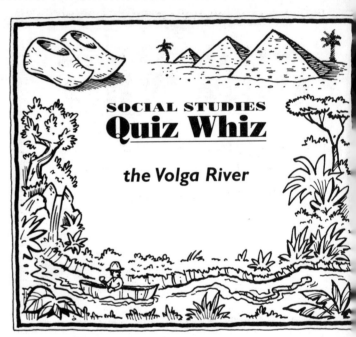

SOCIAL STUDIES
Quiz Whiz

the Volga River

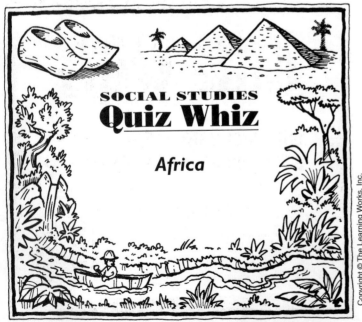

SOCIAL STUDIES
Quiz Whiz

Africa

SOCIAL STUDIES
Quiz Whiz

Norway

SOCIAL STUDIES
Quiz Whiz

What is the largest city and capital of Portugal?

SOCIAL STUDIES
Quiz Whiz

What European volcano erupted in A.D. 79 and buried the city of Pompeii?

SOCIAL STUDIES
Quiz Whiz

Which country is not part of the Middle East: Iran, Angola, Syria, Egypt, or Israel?

SOCIAL STUDIES
Quiz Whiz

If you were in the city of Stockholm, in which country would you be?

SOCIAL STUDIES
Quiz Whiz

On which continent is the Amazon River located?

SOCIAL STUDIES
Quiz Whiz

Which mountain range in Asia is the highest in the world?

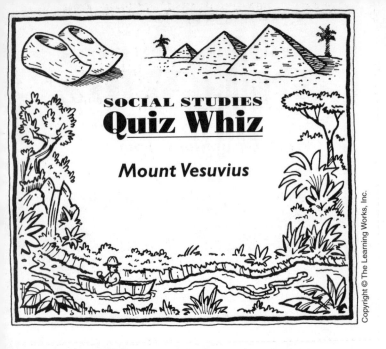

SOCIAL STUDIES
Quiz Whiz
Mount Vesuvius

SOCIAL STUDIES
Quiz Whiz
Lisbon

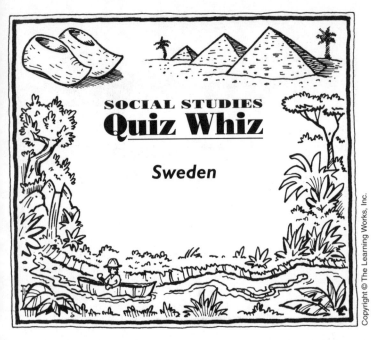

SOCIAL STUDIES
Quiz Whiz
Sweden

SOCIAL STUDIES
Quiz Whiz
Angola

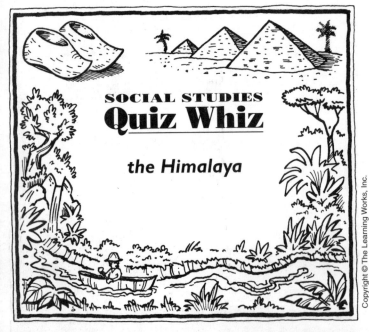

SOCIAL STUDIES
Quiz Whiz
the Himalaya

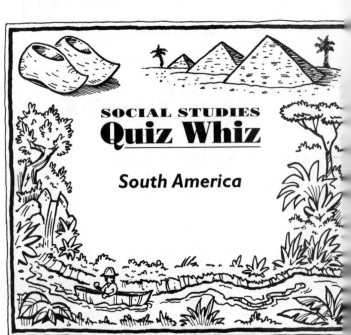

SOCIAL STUDIES
Quiz Whiz
South America